The Common Market

Editor
Julia Kirk
Design
Roland Blunk
Picture Research
Brigitte Arora
Production
Rosemary Bishop
Illustrations
Allard Studios
John Gillatt/Temple Art
Ron Hayward Associates
John Shackell
Consultant
Frances Lawrence, M.A.
University of Sussex

Page 6: the headquarters of the European Communities in the Berlaymont and Charlemagne Buildings in Brussels. The Berlaymont Building (in the shape of a cross) is the home of the Commission. The Charlemagne Building on the left is the home of the Council of Ministers.

Endpaper: January 1 1973 outside the Berlaymont Building in Brussels. Three new flags, those of Britain, Ireland and Denmark, are added to those of France, West Germany, Italy, the Netherlands, Belgium and Luxembourg on the day that the Treaty of Accession becomes official.

Photographic sources
Key to positions of illustrations:
(T) top, (C) centre, (B) bottom, (L) left, (R) right, (M) middle.

L. Armitage : 40(BL)
P. Armitage : 21(TL), 43(TL)
Associated Press : 27(TR), 43(TR)
Australian High Commission : 21(TR)
Belgian Embassy (INBEL) : 35(TR), 38(L) *Belgian National Tourist Office* : 15(TR), 31(TR) *BPC Picture Library* : 15(TL) *Bitburger Brewery* : 19(BR)
British Tourist Authority : 24(BR)
Bundesbildstelle : 31(BL) *Camera & Pen* : 18(TL) *Citroen* : 25(BL) *Commonwealth Institute* : 12(BL) *The Courier* : 42(B)
Daily Telegraph : 39(ML,R), 45(ML)
Danish Tourist Office : 24(BL) *European Communities Commission* : 6, 9(TR,M), 10(BL,M,MR), 13(T,BL), 14(B), 16(TL), 26(BL), 33(TL), 36(TL), 37(BL), 42(TL), 43(B, MR), 60 *European Space Agency* : 47(T) *Foreign Office* : 47(BL) *French Tourist Office* : 29(BR) *Galt Toys* : 41(BL,BR) *German Embassy* : 22(BL), 28(BL), 34(BL)
Daisy Hayes : 26(TL) *Ed Harriman* : 15(BR) *Ingatestone School* : 36(M)
Keystone : 44(BR), 45(ML), 47(MR,BR)
Manpower Services Division : 31(TL)
Antony McAvoy : 41(MR) *Berten van Menen* : 37(BR) *Dennis Moore* : 21(BR)
Mott, Hay & Anderson : 32(TL) *National Centre for Industrial Language Training* : 36(BL) *NBT-Foto* : 12(BR) *Netherlands*

National Tourist Office : 15(BL)
Popperfoto : 13(BR), 44(TL), 45(TL, TR,B), 46(TL,BL) *Post Office* : 25(BR)
Punch : 12(TL) *Rex Features* : 8-9, 25(TR), 32(BR), 33(B), 35(BL,BR) *Ross* : 40(TL) *RSPB* : 38(BR) *Nick Scott* : 37(TL) *Peter Shephard* : 28(TL)
Spectrum : 28(BR) *Erika Sulzer-Kleinemeier* : 21(BL,M) *Syndication International* : 19(BL) *Thames Water Authority* : 39(BL) *Zefa* : 20(BL), 22(TL), 24(TL), 29(TR), 30(BL), 39(TL)

The publishers would also like to thank the European Communities Commission, UK Office, for the help and information they have provided.

First published 1978
Macdonald Educational Ltd.,
Holywell House,
Worship Street,
London EC2A 2EN.
© Macdonald Educational
Limited 1978

ISBN 0 382-06199 3

Published in the United
States by Silver Burdett
Company, Morristown, N.J.
1981 Printing

Library of Congress
Catalog Card No. 78-61095

The Common Market

by
Paul Armitage

Silver Burdett Company

Allen County Public Library
Ft. Wayne, Indiana

7101524

Contents

The ravages of war

Europe in ruins

On May 7 1945, the Second World War ended in Europe with the surrender of the German forces at Rheims in north-eastern France. Europe now lay in ruins. Over 30 million Europeans had died in the fighting. Many more had been injured. There were bombsites everywhere. Many homes, factories, ports, railways and roads had been destroyed and nearly every major European city had been seriously damaged. Industrial and agricultural production fell to very low levels. Many people even faced famine. There was a shortage of fuel and travelling became very difficult. All the Western European countries which had been occupied by Germany were very weak. Britain lost millions of pounds as well as many men in the war effort.

Politically, Europe was split. There were six years of war and many more years of mistrust and hatred between Germany and her European neighbours. And as if this were not enough, differences between the Soviet Union and her former allies now promised yet another split to threaten European peace.

Reconstruction

Europe was in a mess and some quick action was required to deal with its problems.

Some European politicians, including Robert Schuman and Jean Monnet, had been looking at possible solutions even before the war had ended. Their thinking went beyond just looking for solutions to the problems of rebuilding Europe. They also wanted to ensure that such a war would never happen again.

They saw the war basically as a European 'civil war', fought by Europeans among themselves with the rest of the world drawn into the fighting. The cause of the war was, they said, the fact that Europe was split into tiny, individual nations, each representing different national interests. This was bound to lead to rivalry and hatred and then to war.

One country called 'Europe'

So these politicians proposed doing away with independent nation states in Europe and forming one large European 'country'. This would, they hoped, bring several advantages.

First, it would prevent future wars by opening all Europe's resources to all Europeans. There would be no more squabbling over frontiers because these would no longer be important. Also, reconstruction and growth would be speeded up because it would be possible to plan the European economy as a whole.

This, in turn, would bring prosperity to Europe, and make it less likely that people would turn to political extremism of either the left or the right. It would also give Europe more political power in a world which was becoming more and more dominated by the two superpowers, the United States and the Soviet Union.

▼ Europe received a terrible battering during the Second World War. This picture of Alexander Square in East Berlin in 1945 gives you an idea of the extent of the damage. The city suffered in the fierce fighting between German troops defending their capital and the advancing allies.

Europe in 1941

Furthest limit of German advance

Germany

Allies of Germany

Occupied countries

Neutral countries

Great Britain and Protectorates

IRELAND

GREAT BRITAIN

NORWAY

SWEDEN

FINLAND

DENMARK

NETHERLANDS

BELGIUM

LUXEMBOURG

FRANCE

SWITZ

SPAIN

GERMANY

POLAND

SOVIET UNION

HUNGARY

YUGOSLAVIA

RUMANIA

ITALY

GREECE

Black Sea

Mediterranean Sea

▲ Jean Monnet. Born in Cognac, France. In 1943 he was already thinking about a future united Europe. His ideas later formed the basis for his proposals for a European Coal and Steel Community (ECSC).

◄ Every country in Europe was affected by the war. Some countries were occupied by German forces. Many suffered bombing, loss of life and injury. Even 'neutral' states had economic and other difficulties.

▼ Robert Schuman. A Frenchman born in Luxembourg, he later became the French Foreign Minister. He was a keen 'European' and supported Monnet's plans for the ECSC.

The Treaty of Rome

Early unity

It is one thing to say that there should be a country called 'Europe' but quite another to set that country up. In fact, in 1945, most Europeans did not support total unity, and would not consent to the abolition of their own countries. Nor would they agree to their own governments handing over power to one central government ruling the whole of Europe.

But most Europeans did accept that *some* form of cooperation was desirable. This idea was realized in the late 1940s, when three organizations were established: the Organization for European Economic Cooperation (OEEC) to aid economic recovery, the Brussels Treaty Organization (later broadened into NATO) to protect against attack, and the Council of Europe, which would look at cultural and other matters.

The European Coal and Steel Community

But it was not in fact till 1950 that there came the first real step towards unity. This was the publication of the Schuman Plan for a common market in iron, steel and coal produced by member states would be pooled. All member states would be able to buy and use products from the pool as they wished.

One important feature of the proposals was that member states would give up control of their iron, steel and coal industries to a common authority. This authority would have the power to govern all these industries in the member states as one large industry.

Six European nations accepted the plan: France, Germany, Italy, Belgium, Luxembourg and the Netherlands. The United Kingdom did not. It would not give up control of its industry to a central institution. There were therefore six nations that went on to sign the Treaty of Paris, setting up what came to be called The European Coal and Steel Community (ECSC) in April 1951.

The European Economic Community

The success of the ECSC then encouraged the supporters of European unity to propose an extension of the common market in iron, coal and steel to a common market in all products. They saw this as yet another stage towards full political unity. The idea was favourably received by the six ECSC countries at a meeting in Italy in 1955.

A committee under the Belgian, Paul-Henri Spaak, was established to draw up the necessary treaties. It presented its conclusions in May 1956. Intensive negotiations then followed, resulting in a treaty establishing the European Economic Community or the Common Market as it is popularly called. The treaty, signed in Rome on March 25 1957, came to be called the Treaty of Rome. The EEC started working on January 1 1958.

▲ The six founder members of the EEC, who signed the Treaty of Rome on March 25 1957. Britain, Ireland and Denmark joined in 1973.

▼ Paul-Henri Spaak, the Belgian Foreign Minister, seen here facing journalists. It was a committee led by M Spaak that was responsible for the structure of the Common Market as we know it today. His committee wrote the basic text of the Treaty of Rome. This was later approved by the Foreign Ministers of the Six, although they did recommend some changes.

▲ March 25, 1957. The signing of the Treaty of Rome in the Palazzo dei Conservatori on the Capitoline Hill in Rome.

◀ The last page of the Treaty of Rome showing the signatures of the representatives of the six founder members of the EEC. Two ministers from each state signed. Spaak and Snoy et d'Oppuers signed for Belgium, Adenauer and Hallstein for West Germany, Pineau and Faure for France, Segni and Martino for Italy, Bech and Schaus for Luxembourg and Luns and Linthorst Homan for the Netherlands.

The Treaty of Rome

Page 10 shows a photograph of the last page of the Treaty of Rome. From that, it is easy to conclude that the Treaty is both short and simple. In fact, the version printed by the Commission in 1973 runs to 343 pages. It is therefore quite long. It is also quite complicated. Firstly because the language used in treaties is always very dry and official-sounding and secondly because it leaves a lot of the details to be filled in later. So very often the Treaty expresses a general aim for a policy but then leaves it to the politicians of the EEC to work out exactly what the policy will be, and how and when it will work. However, its basic aims are simple and not so difficult to understand. Below are the basic contents of the Treaty in brief form.

General aims

The men who signed the Treaty of Rome hoped that the establishment of the EEC would draw the peoples of Europe closer together. They also hoped it would bring economic growth, improvements in living and working conditions and help to the regions of the Community. Because all the policies of the Treaty could not be introduced at once, a transition period of 12 years was fixed. At the end of this time, the EEC had to be complete.

Customs union

At the end of the 12-year transition period goods crossing borders between member states would no longer be subject to customs duties and other trade barriers. All goods could therefore move freely within the Community. The customs union also meant that at the end of the transition period, all member states would charge a common external tariff—the same customs duties on imports from non-member countries.

Labour mobility

The Treaty said that by the end of the transition period, people from member states should be allowed to go and work anywhere in the EEC. Also, firms could set up business and professional people could offer their services in any member state. Labour mobility (the free movement of people) was to be achieved by gradually ending all restrictions, so that, for instance, work permits would no longer be needed.

Agriculture

The aims of the agricultural policy were to raise productivity and efficiency in farming, to guarantee farmers a reasonable standard of living and to ensure supplies to consumers at reasonable prices. This could be achieved by any measures thought necessary. These would include price controls, loans and technical help to farmers, the retraining and early retirement of farmers' subsidies and common export and import policies.

Transport

If there were to be free movements of goods, services and people in the market, there had to be a common transport policy. Details were not given in the Treaty. They were to be worked out by 1965. But the Treaty did lay down general guidelines. All restrictions on the transport of goods were to be removed, and all rules to do with transport which favoured the companies of one member state over others were to be abolished.

Economic affairs

The member states also agreed to cooperate on their economic policies because, as their economies became linked in the Common Market, what happened in one economy was bound to affect the others. Member states agreed to ensure that all companies in the nine countries would have an equal chance at selling goods throughout all the EEC countries. Monopolies—where a company kept a market for itself—were illegal.

Social affairs

This part of the Treaty was mainly concerned with encouraging the free movement of labour. But the Treaty also wanted to improve living and working conditions. It was also concerned with social security, industrial health and safety, trades union rights, the problems of the unemployed, equal pay for women and paid holidays. The Commission encourages cooperation between the member states in these matters.

Foreign affairs

EEC foreign policy concerns both commerce and association. On commerce, the Treaty stated that it is EEC policy to encourage the development of world trade by the lowering of tariff barriers. On association, the Treaty said that non-member states could become associated with the Community. This applied in particular to the former colonies of member states. It meant that the exports of associate countries could enter the EEC duty free.

Institutions

The Treaty established the institutions which govern the EEC. The Commission sees that the Treaty and all new Community laws are carried out. The European Parliament and the Economic and Social Committee represent the opinions of the peoples of the EEC. The Council is composed of ministers from the member states. They have the final say on what the EEC does. Finally, the Treaty established the Court of Justice which judges infringements of EEC law.

Britain joins the Community

Britain's change of policy

The United Kingdom did not become a member of the Common Market in 1957. Yet within four years of its establishment, she had applied to join and in 1973, she finally became a member. Why did Britain not join in the first place and why did she then change her mind?

The importance of empire

In the 1940s and 1950s, Britain was still a world power with a large empire and trade links with every part of the globe. Both Attlee and Churchill, British Prime Ministers of the period, supported European unity but they saw it as something for continental Europeans, not for the British. They thought it was out of the question that the UK should hand over power to a European super-government which could dictate her policies. So Britain did not join the EEC.

Britain applies for membership

By the 1960s however, the situation facing Britain had changed a great deal. Her economy was relatively weak compared to those of the other members of the EEC. Her empire was fast disappearing and the term 'superpower' was now used only for the USA and the USSR.

So British politicians looked again at the situation and decided that their country's future now lay in a strong, united Europe. In 1961 therefore, the Prime Minister, Harold Macmillan, announced that the UK would apply for membership of the EEC.

No, no then yes

Negotiations on British entry then began and continued until January 1963. It was then, at a famous press conference, that French President Charles de Gaulle declared that France would not allow Britain to join. The British, he said, were not sufficiently 'European minded' and UK entry would, he thought, lead to the destruction of the Community.

For nearly four years, the matter rested. Then, in November 1966, Prime Minister Harold Wilson announced that Britain would again apply for membership. But de Gaulle once more said no.

In 1969, Georges Pompidou became French President. He was known to favour British membership. So it came as no surprise that in December 1969 the Six agreed to open negotiations with Britain and three other applicants – Norway, Denmark and Ireland.

Talks on British entry continued until an agreement was reached in June 1971. The terms of Britain's entry were approved by the British Parliament in October 1971. As a result, she joined the EEC by signing the Treaty of Accession in Brussels in January 1972. It came into force on January 1 1973. Denmark and Ireland joined the EEC at the same time. Norway did not. A referendum (vote) held in Norway showed that the Norwegian people did not wish to join.

▲ Not everyone was pleased about British entry. Many of the Labour Opposition did not like the terms under which Britain was to join the EEC. Here, in this *Punch* cartoon of 1971, Mr Wilson, leader of the Labour Party, joins ex-President de Gaulle in saying 'No' to British entry.

▶ Norway held a referendum to let the people decide whether or not she would join the Common Market. Held on September 24 1972, the referendum showed that the Norwegian people had voted not to join. Here, Prime Minister Trygve Bratteli, accompanied by his wife, makes his way to the polling station.

▼ Prince Charles at Fiji's independence ceremony in 1970. When most of her empire became independent in the 1960s, Britain began taking a much keener interest in Europe.

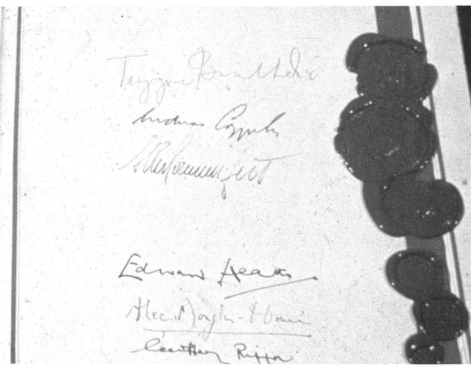

▲ Britain joins the EEC. Here the British Prime Minister, Edward Heath, with Sir Alec Douglas-Home and Mr Geoffrey Rippon, signs the Treaty of Accession in Brussels in January 1972.

◄ The final page of the Treaty of Accession, with the signatures of Heath, Home and Rippon.

▼ Denmark, Ireland and Norway also signed the Treaty of Accession along with the UK, though Norway later decided not to become a member. This picture shows the Danish Prime Minister, Jens Otto Krag, signing the Treaty.

What is the EEC?

The European Community

What exactly is the EEC? Most people refer to it as the Common Market but its correct title is the European Economic Community or EEC. It is one of three Community organizations. The others are the European Coal and Steel Community (ECSC) and the European Atomic Energy Community (Euratom). These are all closely related, are run by the same people in Brussels and together are known as the European Communities or European Community.

Goods, people and money

Let us however concentrate on the EEC or Common Market. By Common Market, we mean an area – in this case France, Italy, West Germany, the UK, Ireland, Belgium, the Netherlands, Denmark and Luxembourg – in which goods, people and money can move about freely as if they are moving within a single country. So French goods can be sold in Italy, Danes can work in Ireland and Dutch money can be invested in Britain, all without restriction. People do not have to pay customs duties on goods when they take them across frontiers between member states, EEC citizens do not need work permits to work in EEC countries and people can transfer money easily from one member state to another.

This then, is what the Common Market is, or at least what the Common Market will be, when all the measures needed to set it up are completed.

More than economics

It may seem that the Common Market has a lot to do with economics. This is true. However, it does go a little further than that. Cooperation in economic matters has encouraged the member states to work together in other areas. So, for instance, member states now cooperate over a whole range of policies. These include social, educational and environmental matters as well as the very important area of foreign policy. Here, however, the process of learning to cooperate is more difficult.

It is becoming clear that the EEC is now moving away from being just a simple common market allowing the free movement of goods, people and money. It could best be described as a group of nine nations attempting to work out their policies together in almost all fields for the benefit of all EEC citizens.

Common identity

The hope of those who set up the EEC was that this cooperation would bring a feeling of common identity to all European people so that, in particular, Europe would never again suffer another world war. To some extent, it is probably true that Europeans do now feel that common identity. So, to complete the definition, one would add that the Common Market now amounts to a collection of 258 million people, all of whom feel themselves to be, in one sense or another, Europeans.

▲ Nine nations today make up the Common Market: France, Germany, Italy, Belgium, Luxembourg, the Netherlands, Ireland, Denmark and Britain.

▼ The EEC covers an area of 1,530,000 square kilometres, and within it live 258 million people, more than in either the USA or the USSR. The value of the goods and services it produces is more than half that of the USA and double that of the USSR. It is the world's largest producer of cars, the world's largest trader and the major importer of goods from the developing nations.

▲ The boulevard café is very common in parts of the Common Market. It is very pleasant to sit on a warm summer day and drink a lemonade, a glass of wine, a beer, or even a cup of tea. Here, people relax outside a café in Belgium.

▼ The EEC is not only interested in economics but also in people and the quality of their lives. Indeed, the EEC's interest in economics comes from its desire to improve the living standards of all its citizens, including those of the old man and the young lady pictured here together in southern Italy.

Many different peoples live within the Common Market's frontiers. There are six official languages: French, English, Danish, Dutch, German and Italian, and many more besides these are spoken in the EEC. Life styles and systems of government vary considerably. For instance, people often associate the British with a love of ceremony and tradition. This picture perhaps bears this out. It shows Prince Charles being invested as Prince of Wales in a ceremony at Caernarvon Castle in 1969. Four EEC countries are monarchies while a fifth, Luxembourg, has a Prince as head of state. The remaining EEC members are all republics with elected presidents. These republics are West Germany, Ireland, Italy and France.

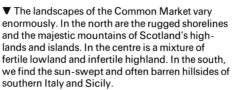 The landscapes of the Common Market vary enormously. In the north are the rugged shorelines and the majestic mountains of Scotland's highlands and islands. In the centre is a mixture of fertile lowland and infertile highland. In the south, we find the sun-swept and often barren hillsides of southern Italy and Sicily.

The photograph here is representative of northern Europe. It shows the Netherlands, a country of flat lands, often below sea level, where rivers and canals are important for drainage, for protection against the sea and for water transport. The soil in the Netherlands, often reclaimed by the Dutch from the sea, is rich and fertile. The result is prosperous agriculture.

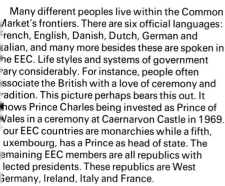

How the Community works

▲ Roy Jenkins, President of the European Commission since January 1977. Once they are appointed, all thirteen commissioners are no longer national representatives: they are responsible to the EEC as a whole. Commissioners are appointed for four-year terms while the President, along with five Vice-Presidents, holds office for two-year, renewable terms.

▼ From start to finish. Seven main stages in the life of a Common Market law.

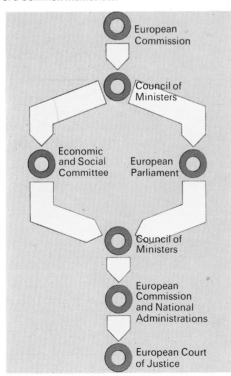

The EEC at work

The European Commission handles the first stage in the planning of any new laws, and its headquarters are in the Berlaymont building in Brussels. The Commission is the 'Civil Service' of the EEC and is composed of about 6000 people, from porters and typists to translators and administrators.

Its job is to propose new laws and then, once these have become Community law, to see that the law is enforced. At its head are 13 Commissioners, two each from the larger member states and one each from the smaller.

One of the Commissioners becomes President of the Commission. The current President is Roy Jenkins, who is British. Once they are appointed, the Commissioners give up their national loyalties and owe allegiance only to the EEC. Roy Jenkins does not represent the United Kingdom, but the European Commission.

The Council of Ministers

A proposed law then passes to the Council of Ministers. This is the body which has the final say on whether or not the proposal becomes Community law. It is composed of nine ministers, each representing their own state.

In reaching its decision, the Council is obliged to consult two bodies. The first is the European Parliament, which is composed of European MPs. The second is the Economic and Social Committee, composed of representatives of trade, industry and other activities. These two bodies represent the people of the EEC.

The proposal becomes law

The Council then goes on to make a decision on whether or not to make the proposal Community law. In practice, all the ministers have to agree before the proposal becomes law. If one minister (and therefore one country) objects, the proposal is usually rejected.

Enforcing the new law is then really the job of the civil services of the member states. This is because the EEC itself does not employ large numbers of administrators in the member states.

If the law is broken, then the Commission will seek to stop this, possibly by taking the matter to the European Court of Justice. This court sits in Luxembourg and is composed of nine judges, one from each member state. The Court can order that the law be respected and punish those who break it.

...L
...ENTS AND
...CAUSE DAMAGE.
...DOES THE EEC
...WITH THIS PROBLEM?

2. THE COMMISSION IN BRUSSELS EXAMINES THE PROBLEM. IT MAKES A PROPOSAL TO LIMIT THE SIZE OF LORRIES IN EEC COUNTRIES.

4. THE ECONOMIC AND SOCIAL COMMITTEE, SEEN HERE HEATEDLY DISCUSSING THE PROPOSAL IN BRUSSELS AND....

5. ..... THE EUROPEAN PARLIAMENT. THIS IS THE BUILDING USED BY THE PARLIAMENT IN STRASBOURG. BUT IT ALSO MEETS IN.....

6. LUXEMBOURG, WHICH IS ALSO THE HOME OF THE PARLIAMENT'S SECRETARIAT.

7. PARLIAMENT THEN DEBATES THE PROPOSAL. TRANSLATORS ARE USED TO OVERCOME THE LANGUAGE BARRIER.

8. THE PROPOSAL THEN GOES BACK TO THE COUNCIL OF MINISTERS FOR A FINAL DECISION.

9. IF THE PROPOSAL IS APPROVED BY COUNCIL, IT BECOMES LAW. IT MUST THEN BE OBSERVED AND ENFORCED BY MEMBER STATES.

10. IF PEOPLE OR MEMBER COUNTRIES BREAK THE NEW LAW, THEN THEY MAY BE TAKEN BEFORE THE EUROPEAN COURT OF JUSTICE AND BE PUNISHED.

Removing barriers to trade

▲ EEC goods can be sold anywhere in the Common Market duty free. Here a lorry carrying goods made in the Netherlands boards a ferry bound for Britain at the Hook of Holland.

▼ Different EEC countries have different laws about cars. For instance, some require special windscreens. Others require special lights. This makes life difficult for the manufacturer and makes cars more expensive. As a result, the EEC is trying to standardize many features on motor vehicles.

The customs union

It was a principal aim of the Treaty of Rome to establish a customs union. The countries of the EEC have agreed to remove all customs duties, quotas and other things which stop or hinder trade between themselves. They have also agreed to set up around themselves a common customs tariff, or tax, to be charged on all goods entering the EEC from outside.

This means that no duties will be charged on goods going from Denmark to Italy. It also means that it is as easy for a French firm to sell its goods in Britain as it is for a British firm. There will be no customs duty to protect and help the British firm and penalize the French. That would be against the spirit of the customs union and law of the EEC.

Prosperity and unity

By creating a customs union, the EEC has created a large market of 258 million people. All firms can now compete on equal terms, encouraging manufacturers to invest money in industry, create jobs, increase production efficiency, lower their costs and pay higher wages. This, in turn, makes people more prosperous so that they can buy more goods. By making the EEC states more dependent on each other for trade, it is hoped that the customs union will also encourage greater unity in other ways between the nine member states.

The full customs union of the Nine is now well on the way to being established. On July 1, 1977, the last remaining customs duties between the member states were removed. Unfortunately, this does not mean that a full customs union has been established because there are still other barriers left which hinder trade. They are known as non-tariff barriers because they do not involve customs duties or tariffs.

Non-tariff barriers

There are many different types of non-tariff barrier but here are examples of only two.

Suppose a French nationalized industry such as electricity always purchases its machinery from French firms. A large part of the French market is then closed to firms from other EEC states while French companies are favoured. This purchasing policy is a barrier reducing or preventing the trade of non-French firms with France.

A second non-tariff barrier concerns tax. Some countries tax goods so that the produce of certain member states is unfairly penalized while the produce of others is not. So wine makers in the EEC claim that by putting high excise duties on wines but a low excise duty on beer, the UK is unfairly discriminating against all wine producers.

The whole problem of non-tariff barriers is a complex one which can only be slowly overcome. Nevertheless, they are gradually disappearing.

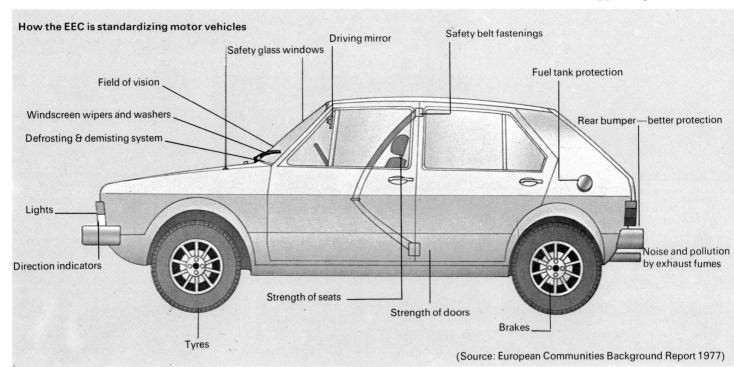

How the EEC is standardizing motor vehicles

Field of vision

Windscreen wipers and washers

Defrosting & demisting system

Safety glass windows

Driving mirror

Safety belt fastenings

Fuel tank protection

Rear bumper—better protection

Lights

Direction indicators

Tyres

Strength of seats

Strength of doors

Brakes

Noise and pollution by exhaust fumes

(Source: European Communities Background Report 1977)

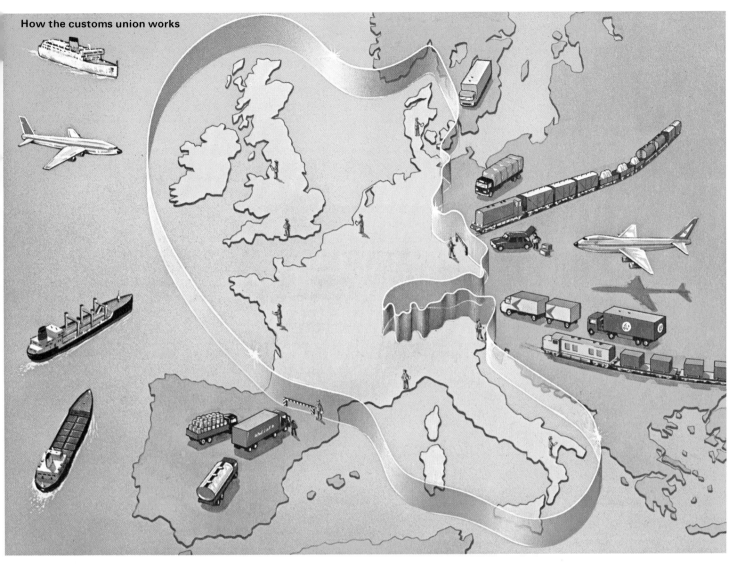

▲ How the customs union works. Standard customs duties are levied on goods coming into the EEC. Goods moving within the EEC travel duty free.

◄ A non-tariff barrier. The EEC wants us to agree on what we mean by ice cream so that firms making cheaper ice cream from vegetable fat will not have an advantage over firms making more expensive ice cream from milk.

▼ Another non-tariff barrier. An old German law says that beer sold there must be made from certain ingredients. Most EEC beer is made differently and so cannot be sold in West Germany.

Free movement for people

Moving within the EEC

The EEC is a common market in goods. It also goes further than that by aiming also at the free movement of the people who produce those goods. This means that the citizens of one member country can now go and work in another member country without much trouble. There is no need to have a work permit.

This at least is the theory, though there are still a number of problems complicating the picture.

The problems of changing countries

Just how easy is it for a person from one member country to go and work in another? How will workers know of job opportunities in the other EEC countries? If an Irishman suddenly becomes redundant six months after going to work in Belgium, can he claim Belgian unemployment pay? Suppose an Italian works for 20 years in Italy and 20 years in Belgium and then he retires in Belgium. Will the Belgians give him a pension which includes the 20 years of contributions paid to the Italian government? What about his trade union and political rights?

Finding a house for his family could be a problem. Can he have a council house? What about finding a suitable school for his children? What about the various language problems facing the migrant and his family? If his mother moves with them, will she continue to receive her old age pension in the new country?

International cooperation

The problem of telling workers about international job opportunities is being solved by an office in Brussels which deals with employment services in the nine member states. Pension and social security contributions made in any EEC state are accepted in all the other member states. Foreign workers also now have the right to join trade unions in their new countries. Family problems are also being solved. Workers can now take all their family with them and in some cases, member states will help with housing.

Language and cultural differences

There are real problems over education. Just how easy would it be for a child from an EEC state to get an education in a foreign city, especially if he or she did not speak the language?

And there are still problems for the professions and trades. In many professions, qualifications differ from one country to another. So the EEC is now encouraging member states to recognize one another's qualifications. Doctors have just made arrangements which allow them to practise in other EEC states but teachers and lawyers still face problems.

The French, for instance, do not encourage the employment of teachers who have not been trained in France and who have not taken French examinations. The differences in the legal systems of the member states also cause obvious problems for lawyers.

▲ A work permit. It is an important aim that EEC nationals should be able to go and work anywhere in the Common Market. Official barriers preventing this, such as work permits, are slowly being removed.

► Official figures for migration *within* the EEC. Going to work in another EEC country poses problems but many thousands have overcome these as the figures show.

▼ Someone who has taken the plunge. A Dutch girl working in Dusseldorf, West Germany.

Movement of workers within the EEC (Source: Economic and Social Committee April 1975)									
COUNTRY OF ORIGIN	COUNTRY OF RESIDENCE								
	B	DK	D	F	IRL	I	L	N	UK
BELGIUM(B)		163	9,568	25,000	9	539	7,200	22,127	7,500
DENMARK(DK)	400		3,062	1,000	24	248	no data	180	2,000
GERMANY(D)	4,500	5,270		25,000	297	7,190	3,800	12,753	71,000
FRANCE(F)	15,000	907	45,821		184	4,145	7,100	1,700	16,500
IRELAND(IRL)	200	414	930	1,000		300	no data	180	452,000
ITALY(I)	90,000	809	297,079	230,000	216		10,400	9,000	72,000
LUXEMBOURG (L)	1,400	5	1,244	2,000	no data	32		60	500
NETHERLANDS (N)	13,500	985	52,488	5,000	85	1,146	600		10,500
UNITED KINGDOM(UK)	5,000	4,298	21,449	11,000	no data	4,500	200	3,800	
TOTAL EEC	130,000	12,851	431,641	300,000	815	18,100	29,300	49,800	630,000

▲ A French 'assistante' (left) teaching in a language laboratory at an English training college. It is now much easier for professional workers to move about in the Community, although they still face difficulties. For example, how many Dutch teachers know enough Danish or French to enable them to go and teach their subjects in Denmark or France? Doctors face similar language problems. Lawyers will have to learn a completely new set of laws and, of course, know the language fluently. It will probably be some time before we see doctors and lawyers moving about easily in the Community.

▶ A classroom scene from the Netherlands. If families are going to be able to move freely within the Common Market, it is essential that there are adequate facilities for the education of children when they arrive in their new country.

▼ Here migrant workers sort out national insurance problems in West Germany. Member states now recognize national insurance contributions paid anywhere in the Community and this certainly encourages labour mobility.

BILDUNGSPOLITIK IN BONN: GEGEN SCHULREFORM U. LEHRERSCHAFT

▲ A family moving to a new job in another EEC country. There used to be serious restrictions on just how many members of his family a worker could take with him when he moved. Now he can take all dependents with him.

◀ A trades union meeting in West Germany. At one time, a migrant worker did not have the same rights as home workers when he moved to a different country in the EEC. Now things have changed. Migrants can vote in trades union elections and stand as candidates for trades union posts.

Farming in the Community

Helping the farmer and the consumer

Agriculture is very important to the EEC, not only to the millions who farm the land but also to the millions of consumers who eat its produce. So the planners of the Treaty of Rome had several things in mind when they drew up what came to be called the Common Agricultural Policy or CAP.

First, there was the need to ensure a reasonable income for farmers, and second, to guarantee an adequate supply of farm produce to consumers at reasonable prices.

To do this, the Commission fixes a level for farm produce below which prices are not allowed to fall. In times of over-production, the Commission buys up and stores excess produce. This prevents its price in the shops from falling and protects the incomes of farmers. This is when we get butter and other food 'mountains'. Later, when production falls off and prices begin to rise, the Commission takes the produce out of store and sells it in the shops, preventing prices from rising too much.

Imports of farm produce are taxed to bring them up to EEC price levels. This stops Community farmers from being put out of business. The revenue from the tax is spent on subsidizing EEC exports of farm produce, making them cheaper for buyers overseas. It is also spent on helping EEC farmers to improve the efficiency of their farms.

The faults of the system

What are the faults of the CAP? The most important is that it leads to consumers in the EEC paying high prices for food. This happens because the EEC has many small and inefficient farms where the cost of producing food is high. So prices have to be high to ensure these farmers a decent living.

This is made worse because people in the EEC cannot enjoy cheaper prices for imported produce, which is taxed when it enters the EEC. In this way, the price of imported goods will not undercut the price charged by the Common Market farmer.

The EEC needs its farmers

But the EEC must keep its farmers and they must receive a decent income. The only real solution to the problem of high EEC prices is to encourage farms to become more efficient with lower costs. This would allow lower prices to be charged for food but would still give farmers a fair standard of living.

The EEC has started tackling this problem. It encourages the development of large farms by pensioning off many owners of smallholdings and paying for the retraining and resettlement of others. The EEC therefore encourages the improvement of farming methods. But it is a policy which involves people who have lived on the land for generations so the policy can only work slowly if it is to be humane.

▲ The agricultural produce of the EEC is very varied, as these three pictures show. This vineyard in southern Italy is only one of thousands in the EEC, which is a large producer of grapes. Most of these go to produce wine.

▶ A herd of Friesian cattle in a field in the Netherlands. Northern Europe is particularly important for its dairy farming.

▼ Threshing corn in West Germany. Although the West German economy has been highly successful, its agriculture, particularly in the south, is not very efficient.

The efficiency of EEC agriculture is variable. In certain areas, such as the Netherlands, Denmark and much of the United Kingdom, it is highly efficient. Farms are mechanized, they employ relatively few people and they produce food cheaply. On the other hand, there are many areas in the EEC, particularly in Italy and West Germany, where farms are small and sometimes split into separate plots, require a lot of people to work them and where the cost of producing food is very high indeed. The result of this has been that consumers have had to pay high prices for food.

Agriculture in the EEC	% country's income provided by farming	% of jobs provided by farming	Size of farms (hectares)	% of total farmland in EEC	% of total EEC farm production
WEST GERMANY	2.5	7.3	13.5	14.2	21.7
FRANCE	4.9	12.0	23.5	33.6	27.6
ITALY	8.3	16.6	7.6	19.1	20.8
NETHERLANDS	4.7	6.6	14.1	2.4	7.8
BELGIUM	2.8	3.7	13.3	1.7	4.0
LUXEMBOURG	2.9	6.6	22.2	less than 1	less than 1
UNITED KINGDOM	2.1	2.8	64.2	20.2	11.7
IRELAND	15.9	24.3	17.7	5.4	2.0
DENMARK	6.0	9.6	22	3.3	4.3

(Source: Basic Statistics of the Community 1975-76)

Industry

Modernizing Europe's industry

There is a great deal in the Treaty of Rome which relates to industry. For instance, the Treaty creates a customs union so that industrial goods produced in the EEC can be sold anywhere in the union without customs duties and other barriers to hinder trade.

It also encourages labour mobility, gives firms the right to set up business anywhere in the EEC and permits the free movement of capital. This means that firms can move money to wherever it is needed and that workers from other EEC states can send money back home.

The Treaty also established the European Investment Bank to provide funds for the modernization of old industries and for the establishment of new ones. Finally, the Treaty states clearly the general desire for economic growth and progress.

Big enterprises

In the early days, the Community said it was very important to try and create larger firms. Firms could then obtain the advantages of large-scale production – higher output and lower prices – and compete on more equal terms with the Americans, Japanese and other industrial nations. So the EEC encouraged mergers between firms, especially between firms in different EEC states because this also helped to cement the EEC together.

The EEC was also very keen on research, especially in the fields of com-puters, transport and metallurgy and lagged behind America and Japan in these fields. Europe's deficiency in computers was thought to be especially serious. Cooperation among EEC member states was intended to help spread the cost of computer research and development and speed up progress.

Greater variety

Recent industrial policy has been more varied. In 1976, for instance, the Community was involved in a detailed study of the structure of EEC industry. It studied such items as the number of jobs, size of production, organization, investment, sales methods and profits, so as to better understand industry and provide a sounder basis for EEC policies. It was also dealing in 1976 with the problems of the EEC steel industry: reduced demand, reduced output, low prices and high unemployment, all of which were a result of the world economic depression.

The EEC has also carried out research into sources of energy for industrial use, especially nuclear energy. Proposals have also been made for developing an EEC aircraft industry and coping with the problems of the EEC's textile and footwear industries. In June 1976, the Commission also produced major proposals aimed at helping the Community's shipbuilding industry through the economic recession of the mid-1970s.

▲ Shipbuilding at the port of Ancona in Italy. The economic recession of the mid-1970s has meant lean times for the Community's shipbuilding industry. Very few orders for ships were placed in 1976. The survival of the shipbuilding industry is vital to the EEC so the member states are now looking at ways to ensure this.

▲ Producing fine china in Denmark. Until quite recently, the EEC has not taken much interest in small and medium-sized businesses. Now the EEC has started asking how it may help them. The answer seems to be with money and advice.

► Concorde – the combined effort of the French and British aircraft industries. Producing new aircraft is very expensive so the EEC is keen to develop a joint industry involving all EEC states.

Industrial production in the EEC—1975

	Crude steel (thousand tonnes)	Motor vehicles (thousands)	Merchant ships (thousands tonnes)
W. GERMANY	40,415	3,191	2,549
FRANCE	21,530	3,293	1,301
ITALY	21,837	1,459	847
NETHERLANDS	4,826	86.5	951
BELGIUM	11,584	858	211
LUXEMBOURG	4,624	0	0
UNITED KINGDOM	19,780	1,648	1,305
IRELAND	81	39	28
DENMARK	558	1.5	961

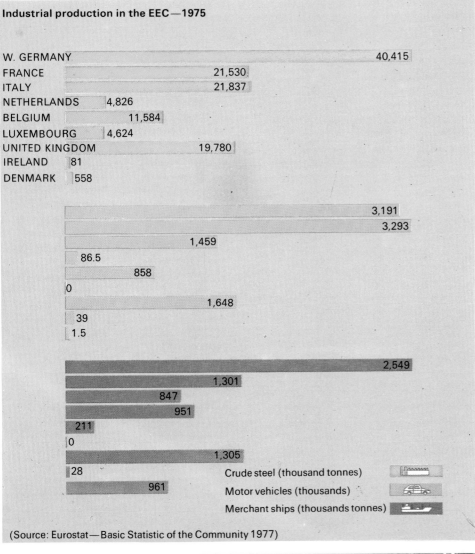

(Source: Eurostat—Basic Statistic of the Community 1977)

◀ This chart shows the production of three selected goods in 1975. West Germany produced more steel and ships than any other member and France produced more cars. Luxembourg's industrial production is small, but then she is only a small country. The low output on these goods by Denmark and Ireland perhaps reflects their bias towards agriculture.

▼ Steel being produced in the EEC. The effects of the 1970s recession have been greater on steel than on any other industry.

▲ A computer in operation at the British Post Office's London Computer Centre. The EEC has been worried by the American domination of the computer industry. In 1974, the Community began a major programme so that by 1980, Europe would have a computer industry of its own.

◀ Citroen cars in production. The oil crisis and the depression of the 1970s hit the car industry hard. Demand for cars has now picked up but it is still down on the 1960s. To help solve the difficulties, the Commission has proposed a Community programme to improve productivity, carry out research and increase sales.

25

Building a strong economy

▲ How much can I get for my pound note? This board, photographed in a bank, will tell you. Exactly how much you get varies from day to day.

► How prices have risen in the Community in the 1970s – the example of Britain. Inflation has been felt in all member states and has made it very difficult to develop a coordinated EEC economic policy.

▼ Nine different currencies in the nine member states. Life would be very much simpler if there were a single European currency.

Controlling the economy

Economic union in the EEC means that all member states are dependent upon one another's economies and are affected by them. Here is an example. Suppose West Germany is suffering from high unemployment. Its government may decided to 'inflate' its economy. In other words, it will encourage people to spend more money, so giving more work to firms who will then employ more people. This inflation of the economy will also mean more work for people in other countries, because Germans will now buy more goods from abroad.

Supposing now, however, that West Germany runs into trouble with rising prices and low export sales. It may then decide to 'deflate' the economy. This in turn will result in less work and maybe even unemployment for people in other countries because the Germans now reduce their buying overseas.

Working together

This example shows how the policies of one country can affect others. For instance, it matters a great deal to Italian refrigerator makers if the British or French economies are strong or weak. If they are weak, it means fewer sales of Italian refrigerators in those countries and therefore higher unemployment figures in Milan and other centres of production.

So in the Rome Treaty, member states of the EEC agreed to consult one another and the Commission on economic policy. This would help to solve economic problems in the interests of all member states, and not just the member state affected.

Monetary union

By the end of the 1960s, however, it was becoming obvious that the EEC's attempts to link the economic policies of member states were not being successful. Countries were still putting their own interests before the interests of all. And this was becoming increasingly serious. Because as the Common Market grew older, so member states became more and more dependent on one another's economies. So the policies of any one member state had increasingly important effects on the others.

Also, at this time, there was growing interest in the idea of monetary union. That is to say that the EEC should have a single currency. If this was to be arranged, there would have to be very close agreement about economic matters. So with all this in mind, the member states of the EEC decided to increase economic cooperation.

Unfortunately, things have still not gone well. The prosperity of the EEC in the 1960s has given way to the depression of the 1970s. Agreeing on economic policies has been difficult, and the aim of a single currency by 1980 now seems impossible.

How prices have risen

European Investment Bank loans—1975
% of total

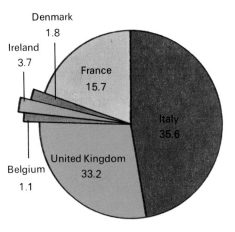

Denmark
1.8
Ireland
3.7
France
15.7
Italy
35.6
Belgium
1.1
United Kingdom
33.2

(Source: EEC Commission)

▲ The above chart shows how European Investment Bank loans were distributed in 1975. Notice how Italy, with its relatively poor economy, received the lion's share of over 35% of all loans made by the Bank. And the United Kingdom with its 33.2% was not far behind. Notice how Ireland, Belgium and Denmark received only a small percentage of the total loaned. The fact that they are relatively small countries with small populations had something to do with this. Finally, notice how West Germany, Luxembourg and the Netherlands received no loans at all, largely because of their relative wealth and prosperity.

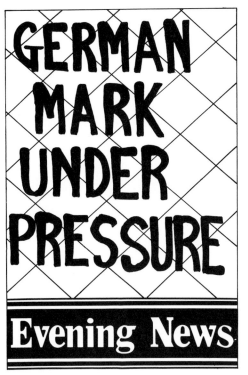

GERMAN MARK UNDER PRESSURE

Evening News

▲ A newspaper placard announces an unusual event — a bad day for the West German mark. The West German economy has been one of Europe's strongest since the 1950s and therefore the value of its currency compared with others has been high.

▲ A dole queue in Northern Ireland. Dole is another word for unemployment pay. The length of this queue is exceptional. Special problems in Northern Ireland have caused a lot of unemployment. Nevertheless, it is a typical picture from the 1970s. The number unemployed in all the member states of the Community has soared and the EEC has been looking at ways of reducing unemployment. Because most people's jobs are dependent one way or another on foreign trade, it is now generally agreed that cooperation, both between member states of the EEC and between the EEC and other nations, is the only way to end the depression and reduce unemployment.

▼ A graph to illustrate the so-called European currency 'snake'. When the values of currencies are plotted, the result looks something like a snake. In 1970, the member states aimed to introduce a single currency by 1980. There would then be neither pounds nor francs. As a first stage towards union, member states agreed to link their currencies together so that one mark, for instance, would always exchange for the same number of guilder. However, because of the economic depression, it has proved very difficult to hold currency exchange rates stable. Some EEC countries could not even join the Snake and others, such as France, have been forced to leave.

The 'Snake'—linking currencies together

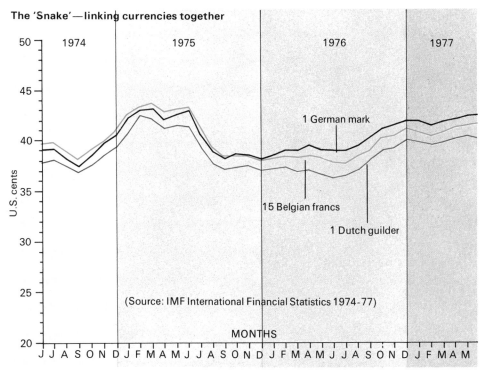

1974   1975   1976   1977

1 German mark

15 Belgian francs

1 Dutch guilder

U.S. cents

(Source: IMF International Financial Statistics 1974-77)

MONTHS

J J A S O N D J F M A M J J A S O N D J F M A M J J A S O N D J F M A M

Transport – the vital link

The vital role of transport

The Common Market is a common market for goods, and the EEC is interested in any policy that will help to create and maintain that large market. The Community considers a well-developed transport system to be essential for economic unity between the nine member states and transport therefore has a vital role to play in this because it carries goods to all parts of the Community.

The Rome Treaty said there should be a common transport policy but said very little about how this policy would work. Instead, it was left to the Commission to outline a policy in 1961.

This policy had three main aims: first, to get rid of any difficulties which transport can put in the way of creating a common market; second, to introduce policies to encourage the growth of trade between member states; third, to introduce policies which would help to create healthy competition between firms.

Encouraging competition

In the 1960s, the EEC concentrated on encouraging fair competition between firms. So, it became illegal in certain circumstances for a member state to subsidize railway transport. This could give an unfair advantage to its own companies if other member states did not do the same for their firms.

An agreement was also reached in 1969 on charges for road haulage, in order to ensure fair competition throughout the EEC. It also became illegal for a member state to keep either some routes or some types of transport for its own people. Such matters as the conditions of employment of lorry drivers, their age in relation to lorry size and the number of hours a driver can drive before resting were also settled, again to make sure that all firms in the EEC are treated alike.

Wider horizons

In 1973 there came a new set of guidelines for transport. The EEC would continue to create a common transport market but also had broader developments in mind. This has resulted in fixing standards of roadworthiness and the weights and dimensions of commercial vehicles. Suggestions have even been made for an EEC driving licence.

The EEC aims to encourage trade and to reduce costs, and efforts have been made to try to agree on transport building programmes. This means that the EEC has taken a major interest in national motorway building plans and is generally in favour of such projects as the Channel Tunnel.

The 1973 guidelines have also resulted in greater efforts to understand the transport needs of the EEC. There have been detailed cost studies of road, rail and water transport. Air transport facilities have been looked at and a study has been made of passenger transport needs between large cities.

▲ Since 1975, the Commission has been looking into the rates charged by air companies to see if rates conflict with the EEC's rules about unfair trading competition.

▶ Europoort, Rotterdam. A Working Party on ports was established by the EEC in 1974 to obtain a clearer picture of their organization and problems.

▼ A barge carries goods on the River Rhine. Should the EEC do more to encourage firms to transport goods by canal and river?

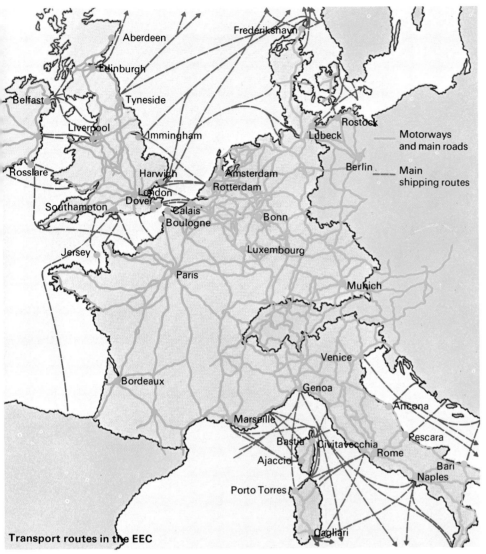

Transport routes in the EEC

Motorways and main roads

Main shipping routes

▲ What would happen if Europe's motorways did not meet? Imagine what would happen if the French built a motorway to the German frontier without telling the Germans. The EEC wants to see even more cooperation between member states in transport matters with the aim of creating a unified transport system.

◀ Transport has a major role to play in creating and maintaining the Common Market. It is EEC lorries, cars, buses, ships, barges, trains and aircraft that carry goods and people to all nine member states.

◀ Still an exciting idea, the Channel Tunnel would mean easier movement for people and goods between the UK and the Continent. The project is too expensive for Britain and France alone to undertake but the EEC as a whole could possibly afford it.

▼ The railways of Europe all make a loss and have to be subsidized by their governments. The EEC has to ensure that this financial aid does not break competition rules. If one member state subsidizes freight transport and other states do not, this can give firms in that country an unfair advantage.

Looking after the people

▲ The EEC shows a keen interest in safety, hygiene and health protection at work. It wants to reduce the number of accidents at work and reduce risks to workers who deal with dangerous substances.

▶ The Community finances the construction, modernization and purchase of houses for workers in the coal, iron and steel industries. The chart shows how much was spent in this way between 1954 and 1975.

▼ The Treaty of Rome requires member states to see that men and women receive equal pay for equal work. Progress in this has been faster in some countries than in others.

Looking after the people

The social policies of the member states of the EEC are mainly a matter for those states. It is the individual governments who decide how much money their people should pay in tax and how much should be spent on hospitals, schools and pensions.

But the EEC does have an interest in the social policies which will contribute to the creation of a common market. So certain policies have been worked out by all the member states as a whole. There have been policies to standardize such things as work conditions in factories, trade union rights, bonus systems and paid holidays throughout the EEC.

The aim has been to make sure that all workers and all companies in the EEC are treated alike. In this way, the goods produced in one member state are not made more expensive than similar goods produced in other member states.

Social policy has also aimed at encouraging the movement of people by encouraging member states to accept one another's national insurance contributions. This means, for instance, that France will pay the retirement pension of a worker even if that worker has worked for a time in Britain and has paid contributions to the British government.

New directions

Since 1974 the social policy of the FEC has broadened. This new attitude has brought several benefits, including, for instance, more help for workers who move to other EEC countries. Safety at work has been emphasized, equal pay for men and women doing the same job has been encouraged and greater help is now provided for people made redundant. EEC policies have also encouraged the provision of more vocational training and help to the handicapped. In addition, steps have been taken to improve the living conditions of non-EEC people working in the EEC, many of whom live in very poor housing conditions.

There have also been various studies. One looked at the possibility of standardizing retirement age. Others have looked at the special problems of low-paid workers, of miners and of fishermen. Since 1974, special attention has been given to dealing with high unemployment in the EEC. Grants are now provided from the European Social Fund for the retraining of unemployed workers, and there have been special policies to deal with the problems of unemployed young school leavers.

Effective or not?

Some of these policies have been very effective. For instance, the ability to transfer national insurance contributions from one country to another has been very important in encouraging people to find jobs abroad. Other policies, such as those aimed at improving the living conditions of migrants or dealing with the problems of the unemployed, have not had much effect.

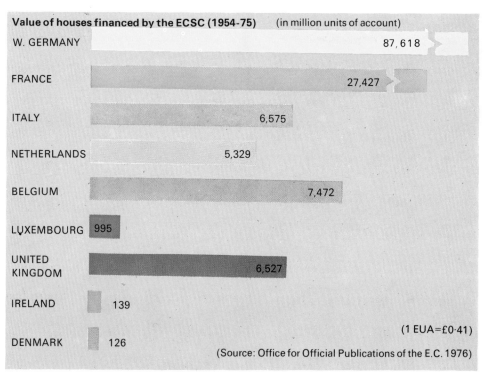

Value of houses financed by the ECSC (1954-75)   (in million units of account)

W. GERMANY	87,618
FRANCE	27,427
ITALY	6,575
NETHERLANDS	5,329
BELGIUM	7,472
LUXEMBOURG	995
UNITED KINGDOM	6,527
IRELAND	139
DENMARK	126

(1 EUA = £0·41)

(Source: Office for Official Publications of the E.C. 1976)

▲ Redundant workers learning new skills. The EEC provides money to help unemployed people to retrain so that they can find new jobs.

► Everyone likes paid holidays. These are specifically mentioned in Article 120 of the Rome Treaty. Though it is unlikely that it will be achieved in the near future, the ideal would be for all people in the EEC to get at least four weeks paid holiday a year.

► The economic depression of the middle 1970s has been accompanied by high unemployment, as these figures show. The EEC has been concerned both because of the personal problems unemployment brings to the people concerned and because it is a serious waste of manpower. The EEC has given help to specific industries and also to individual workers to retrain and move to other parts of the Community.

▼ In 1974, the Council approved the first Community action programme for the vocational training of handicapped persons.

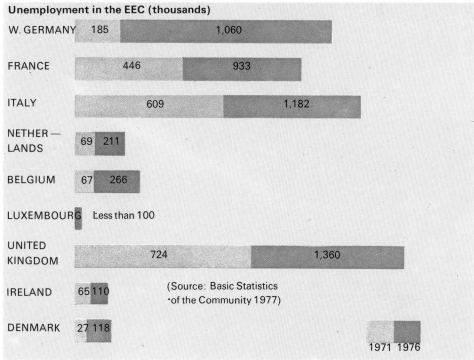

Unemployment in the EEC (thousands)

	1971	1976
W. GERMANY	185	1,060
FRANCE	446	933
ITALY	609	1,182
NETHERLANDS	69	211
BELGIUM	67	266
LUXEMBOURG	Less than 100	
UNITED KINGDOM	724	1,360
IRELAND	65	110
DENMARK	27	118

(Source: Basic Statistics of the Community 1977)

1971 1976

Help for the regions

Why we need a regional policy

In the Common Market countries there are some areas which are poorer than others and where people have less money and a lower standard of living. Sometimes these are agricultural areas where the land is infertile, where the farms are small and where there is little money for improvements.

In other cases they are industrial areas where old industries have declined and new industries have failed to take their place. Then there are special areas such as Northern Ireland and the border areas between West and East Germany where political problems mean that businessmen do not want to invest there.

Helping all the regions

Governments have for a long time struggled with the problems of these areas. The EEC had to create a regional policy because it was interested in improving the living and working conditions of all its citizens and because of the large number of problem regions. There was also the problem that if something was not done for these regions, their relative poverty would get worse. People would leave to work elsewhere in the EEC and businessmen would invest their money in neighbouring, rich areas. This would create some very rich areas and others of great poverty. Besides being unfair, this would threaten the aim of political unity.

Nearly all EEC policies have taken regional problems into account. Social policy, for instance, will help with the retraining and resettlement of unemployed workers from old industries. Agricultural policy provides money for farm investment and transport policy can also help in deprived areas.

The Regional Development Fund

Although there has been a great deal of aid to the regions, it was decided in 1975 that even more planning was necessary. The result was the creation of a Regional Development Fund, to be spent on approved projects in the regions. This can help in various ways. It can aid the establishment of new industry and the modernization of the old, the building of such things as roads and power lines, and it can also help agriculture in certain ways. The money is divided among member states according to need. So far, Italy has received the most, followed by Britain and then France.

To date, the EEC's regional policy has had mixed success. Aid has been considerable and some regions have advanced as a result. But the EEC admits that generally this aid has not been enough. The economic depression of the 1970s has made regional problems worse. Unemployment has increased, especially in the problem regions. The EEC has tried to solve this problem by making various proposals, which include increasing the size of the Regional Development Fund. It remains to be seen just how effective these proposals will be.

▲ The Dartford Tunnel under the Thames, England. The European Investment Bank also finances projects which are not in backward regions, but which, because of their size or special character, could not be financed by a single member state. Thus it has provided funds for the modernization of the Mont Cenis rail link between Paris and Genoa, and for the improvement of the road tunnel under the River Thames at Dartford in England. The bank can also make loans to developing nations. Greece, Turkey and some African states have all received substantial sums.

▶ Calabria in southern Italy. The whole of southern Italy is a poor region and incomes are very low. They are below the national average for Italy and well below incomes in the more prosperous parts of the EEC. The reason is that there is very little industry and agriculture is poor and unproductive. As a result of this lack of economic opportunity, many southern Italians migrate to other parts of Europe. The EEC provides funds and policies to help regions such as these to become more prosperous.

Regions which receive aid from the European
Regional Fund. Notice how it is the regions on the
edge of the Community which are the problem
areas and which receive money. Notice too the
other areas that do not qualify for aid from the
Fund.

The European Investment Bank's headquarters
Luxembourg. The Bank makes interest-free
loans throughout the Community. It has a
particularly important role in the backward regions
where it finances development projects.

Grants to the member states from the Regional
Development Fund. The way the Fund is split
between member states depends on the size of
their regional problems. Italy gets 40% of the money
in the Fund. The UK gets 28% and France 15%. All
the other member states each get less than 6.5%.

One of the richest regions in Europe — the Paris
Basin. The EEC wants to see a more equal
distribution of wealth in the EEC so that these
pockets of extreme wealth and poverty no longer
exist.

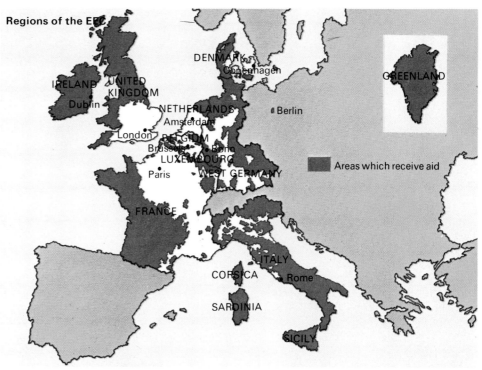

Regions of the EEC

Areas which receive aid

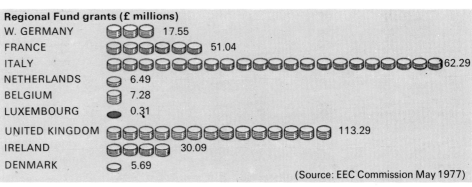

Regional Fund grants (£ millions)

W. GERMANY	17.55
FRANCE	51.04
ITALY	362.29
NETHERLANDS	6.49
BELGIUM	7.28
LUXEMBOURG	0.31
UNITED KINGDOM	113.29
IRELAND	30.09
DENMARK	5.69

(Source: EEC Commission May 1977)

Supplying the EEC's energy needs

The energy crisis of the 1970s

There was no mention of the need for a common energy policy in the Treaty of Rome. However, it soon became apparent that one was needed. There were problems facing the EEC's coal industry in the 1950s and 1960s caused, in particular, by the increase in the use of oil.

So in 1964 came the first EEC energy policy. It aimed at providing the consumer with cheap, secure energy supplies. It gave special help to the coal industry, which was suffering because of the popularity of oil. The new policy involved such things as the reorganization of the coal-mining industry and the storage of oil.

But the new policy was not very successful and the oil crisis of the 1970s soon showed that there were many weaknesses. For instance, the crisis proved that the Community's energy supplies were very insecure. Also, her own energy resources, such as nuclear energy, North Sea oil and gas, were very under-developed. The crisis also showed how coal had been neglected as a source of power. Above all, it showed how important it was for member states to agree on their energy policies.

The Copenhagen Conference

So in December 1973, a conference of Heads of State from the EEC member states was held at Copenhagen to examine the problems. It was decided that there should be a new energy policy. Member states should cooperate to reduce the demand for energy in the EEC. They decided that other sources of energy, apart from oil, should be developed and that member states should agree on a joint policy towards the oil-supplying countries.

Towards a common policy

Since that time, the Commission has studied the demand for energy, so that it now more clearly understood. An Energy Committee has been established to make sure that member states agree on what action they should take. The Commission has stressed again the need to develop new energy sources and has suggested various ways of reducing energy consumption. It has also studied the problem of the energy industry and how more money can be invested in it.

But although these measures have been useful, an agreed common energy policy has not yet been worked out. At the Council of Ministers meeting in March 1976, the Ministers decided that a common energy policy was necessary. However, they could not agree on what this policy should be. They could not decide on what to do in a crisis. Nor could they agree on what action they should take to help the development of the EEC's own energy resources.

Since reliable sources of energy are vital to the EEC countries, the Ministers' failure to agree is worrying. It also shows how far the EEC must progress towards achieving common policies.

A watched kettle never boils away.

Forgetting to turn those little things off wastes £s. SAVE IT

▲ Because of the shortage of energy and its high cost, EEC member states have mounted publicity campaigns to encourage people to save energy.

▶ Energy consumption in the EEC compared with selected foreign states. The EEC is the world's third largest consumer of energy after the USA and the USSR.

▼ Between 1945 and the crisis of the 1970s, the coal industry was run down as people turned to oil as a source of power. Now that oil supplies are running out, the EEC is looking to its huge coal resources for the future.

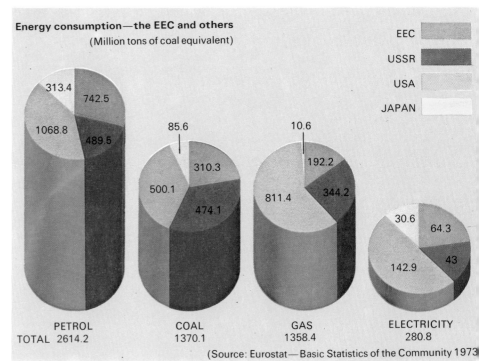

Energy consumption—the EEC and others
(Million tons of coal equivalent)

EEC
USSR
USA
JAPAN

PETROL
TOTAL 2614.2

313.4
742.5
1068.8
489.5

COAL
1370.1

85.6
310.3
500.1
474.1

GAS
1358.4

10.6
192.2
811.4
344.2

ELECTRICITY
280.8

30.6
64.3
142.9
43

(Source: Eurostat—Basic Statistics of the Community 1973)

▶ The Belgian Nuclear Energy Study Centre near Antwerp, with its three large reactors. Nuclear energy is important to Europe. Since the start of the crisis there has been a determined effort by the EEC to develop it.

▼ Even before 1973, there were signs that there would soon be an energy shortage in the EEC. But it was the Yom Kippur war of 1973 which made Europeans realize just how insecure their energy resources were. The Arabs reduced oil supplies to the EEC in an attempt to force the nine member states to put pressure on Israel to withdraw from Arab territory. The EEC is now developing its own oil supplies.

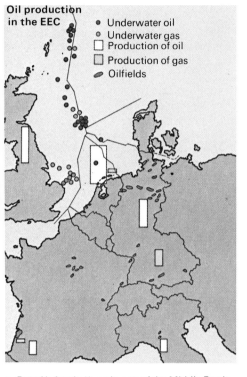

Oil production in the EEC

- ● Underwater oil
- ○ Underwater gas
- ▢ Production of oil
- ▢ Production of gas
- ⬭ Oilfields

▶ Petrol is free in Kuwait, one of the Middle East's main producers of oil. In 1973, the Arab oil-producing countries reduced oil supplies to Western Europe, causing severe economic problems. As a result, the Community began thinking seriously about its energy policies. Where will the EEC get its energy when Arab oil finally stops flowing?

▼ Energy prices have soared in the 1960s. Scientists have started looking around for alternative energy sources. In this case solar energy gives light and heat to this building in France.

Education and training

Educating for Europe

As with social policy, education is not the responsibility of the EEC. It is not the EEC's job to run schools, decide on what is taught, or train teachers. Nowhere in the Rome Treaty is there any mention of education. However, there is now an education policy, though for the moment it is a comparatively minor one.

The basis for the education policy was a set of proposals from the Commission to the Council of Ministers in March 1974. The proposals said that there should be no attempt to make the education systems of the member states the same, but it would be useful to have certain common aims.

First, the Commission suggested that the people of the EEC should be helped to understand one another better. This could be achieved by encouraging the study of Europe and Europeans, by improving the teaching of foreign languages and by increasing links between schools in different parts of the EEC. The Com-

mission also called for more opportunities for teachers and students to work in other EEC countries. This would mean that the qualifications of one country should be accepted in all the member states and that scholarships and training schemes available in one EEC country should be open to all EEC students.

Second, the Commission said there should be better facilities for children who migrate with their families to different parts of the EEC. This would include special training in the language and culture of their new country. Facilities should also be provided to enable them to continue their education in their mother tongue and to prepare them for an easy return to school in their own country.

The 'action programme'

From these proposals came, in February 1976, an 'action programme' agreed by the Ministers of Education of the Nine. This was a decision to put into practice the Commission's proposals.

▲ Nine children from the nine member states of the EEC. The EEC has created an education policy for three main reasons. First, to help foster a feeling of unity among European peoples, especially the young. Second, to give the people of the EEC a better understanding of what is going on in the Common Market so that they can play a bigger role in its government. Third, to encourage labour mobility by helping people to feel at home in all parts of the EEC. The Ministers of Education of the Nine have agreed that all schools should be encouraged to teach more about Europe – and this means teaching about the whole of Europe, not just the EEC countries.

▲ The EEC also takes an interest in the education of adults and the education of immigrants. Here laundry workers in the UK learn English at a course organized by the National Centre for Industrial Language Training. The EEC puts up some of the money to pay for the Centre's work.

▶ An unhappy teacher on a boat crossing from Calais to Dover. Official EEC policy supports exchange visits between schools. It would like to see them become easier and cheaper to organize. If the EEC has its way, such scenes as this will be seen more often!

◀ One school which thinks that children should study both Europe and the world at large is the Anglo-European school at Ingatestone in Essex. This County Council Comprehensive School has a special curriculum which encourages the detailed study of Europe. Field trips are an especially important part of the school curriculum. Here, two older pupils are seen answering work sheet questions in the West German town of Saulgau. The EEC, together with many teachers, politicians and businessmen, would like to see other schools following Ingatestone's example so that European children learn more about their continent and its people.

▲ Recently, as a result of the high numbers of unemployed school-leavers, the Ministers of Education of the Nine have been paying special attention to the need to properly train young people at school for working life. The subjects taught should be changed if necessary to make them more relevant to the world today. Here, a 15 year-old Italian student at a professional training school in Rome learns how to type.

▶ Numbers of pupils and students in the EEC. In addition to these figures, a further 7½ million children were in nursery schools. Of these, 2½ million were in France.

Numbers of pupils and students in the EEC (thousands)

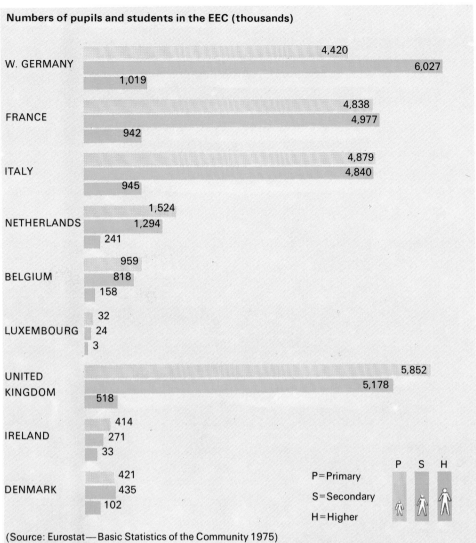

W. GERMANY
4,420
6,027
1,019

FRANCE
4,838
4,977
942

ITALY
4,879
4,840
945

NETHERLANDS
1,524
1,294
241

BELGIUM
959
818
158

LUXEMBOURG
32
24
3

UNITED KINGDOM
5,852
5,178
518

IRELAND
414
271
33

DENMARK
421
435
102

P = Primary
S = Secondary
H = Higher

(Source: Eurostat — Basic Statistics of the Community 1975)

▲ Children of all nationalities at the European School in Luxembourg. There are a few of these schools in Europe which provide special facilities for children so that they can do their lessons in most major west European languages. In this way, many of them become competent linguists and they feel at home with children from all Common Market states.

▶ Children learning how to bake at a vocational training school in the Netherlands. If this training is not to be wasted, it should only be given for those jobs where we know there will be vacancies.

Protecting the environment

A materialistic EEC?

The early years of the Common Market were very much concerned with establishing the free movement of goods, money and people – the main features of the Common Market. But although economics have much to do with the prosperity and happiness of people, many people felt that the EEC was far too preoccupied with material things and that it cared far too little for the real quality of life of its citizens.

Therefore, the politicians of the EEC began looking at policies which would have an immediate and direct effect on the quality of life of the people in the Community.

Improving our environment

So in November 1973, the Council of Ministers approved an environmental 'action programme'. The aim of this was 'to improve the setting and quality of life and the surroundings and living conditions of the people of the Community'. In particular, the Commission wanted to achieve four things: to prevent and eliminate pollution where possible; to maintain the ecological balance; to use natural resources without unnecessary destruction and to persuade planners to consider the environment.

From this has come a variety of measures. For example, the Council of Ministers has approved very strict measures to protect the Mediterranean Sea and the River Rhine from further pollu-

tion. The Mediterranean is in grave danger of becoming a great 'drain' for the rubbish from adjoining countries. The Rhine is also heavily polluted.

The programme has involved a number of studies. The danger levels of certain harmful chemicals such as mercury have been investigated and air pollution has been studied. Attempts have also been made to fix the minimum quality of water for drinking, bathing and shellfish breeding. Scientists have also been investigating other problems: for example, the disposal of industrial waste from factories and methods of protection against nuclear radiation.

The lessons of Seveso

The tragic disaster at Seveso in northern Italy in 1976 brought the matter of protecting the environment to the public attention. An explosion at a chemical-making factory caused the surrounding countryside to be showered with a poisonous chemical. Following this, the Commission said there should be stricter controls over the manufacture of dangerous substances.

The Commission has also signed on behalf of member states a number of international agreements relating to the environment. In 1976, these included an international agreement relating to the pollution of seas and other international watercourses, and the Washington Convention, limiting international trade in rare plants and animals.

Non aux villes inhumaines!...

▲ A poster concerned about the quality of life in Europe's towns and cities. This is one of the things which the European Foundation for the Improvement of Living and Working Conditions, recently established by the EEC in Dublin, will have to consider.

▶ A sea bird covered in oil. The EEC has taken steps to prevent the contamination of the sea with oil and other substances. In 1976, it also suggested measures to protect endangered species of wild birds.

▲ Noise and air pollution from an aircraft. These alone are quite bad enough but there is another danger to the environment. Birds on airfields may endanger aircraft. Worms in airfield grass attract the birds. So organochlorine poisons are used to kill the worms. These poisons may harm the environment so the EEC wants their use restricted.

▲ Loud noise pollutes the environment quite as much as smoke and rubbish. So in addition to encouraging the member states to tighten up on noise, the Commission has also suggested some possible limits.

► Atmospheric pollution by industry. In an attempt to improve the quality of the air we breathe, the EEC has policies aimed at reducing pollution by cars, aircraft, factories and domestic consumers.

▼ Testing the quality of the water in the Thames estuary in Britain. The EEC has policies aimed at reducing the pollution of Europe's rivers. It also has policies which strictly control the quality of the water we use for drinking and other purposes.

Helping the consumer

Protecting the consumer

The EEC is concerned with people as well as politics and economics. One example of this is the development since 1975 of a consumer protection policy. This has resulted in a number of important measures, all of which aim to protect and help people in various ways.

For instance, certain chemicals used for colouring food have been banned because they are thought to be harmful to human health. Nine such chemicals were banned in 1976.

Other dangerous elements in food have also been closely studied. One example is the chemical erucic acid. It is found in vegetable oils made from mustard seeds. If people consume too much of it, it will cause heart disease. Therefore, the Council of Ministers has stated the maximum amount of the acid allowable in vegetable oils.

Safeguarding the quality of food

The EEC is also preparing various measures to improve hygiene in meat chilling factories and to tighten up on checks to see that imported meat is fit for human consumption. The EEC has also attempted to safeguard the quality of ice cream throughout the member states. For instance, the Commission wants consumers to be sure that they are getting a product made from milk and not vegetable fat when they ask for ice cream.

Other matters which the EEC has turned its attention to include the stan-dardized labelling of textiles with clear instructions on care and cleaning; greater toy safety; an end to all misleading advertising and the unit pricing of foodstuffs so that consumers can tell which brand or packet is the best value for money.

Clear labelling for food

The Commission also wants the clear and useful labelling of foods. Labels should include ingredients, last date for consumption, method of preserving and the names of both manufacturer and sellers.

The latest EEC consumer protection policy to be announced concerns eggs. There are now to be seven sizes or grades of egg. The consumer will have a better idea of the size of egg he is buying instead of only the rough idea he had when there were fewer grades, and prices will be fairer.

Consumer organizations

The EEC is not the only body involved in protecting the consumer. In addition to the governments of the member states, there are many private consumer organizations involved. The EEC has worked with them in deciding on its proposals and it has given many of them money to pay for studies. These range from inquiries into food prices to studies on the advertising and sale of drugs.

The EEC also takes the view that consumers can do a lot to help themselves and so has begun a programme of consumer education for both children and adults.

▲ Poultry chilling. Using a defective process might mean that people could end up with food poisoning. So, the EEC strictly controls the processes used by chilling factories.

▶ Faulty products? EEC policy ensures that makers take responsibility both for the faulty products and any damage or injury resulting from them.

▼ *Trichinella,* less than 1 mm long, are sometimes found in uncooked pork, and cause disease. A new Commission proposal seeks to improve the inspection of pork to see that infected meat is not sold.

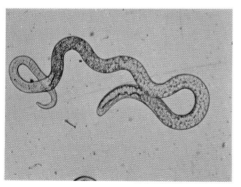

This carton contains 3 sachets

1. Pastry Mix
2. Lemon Filling Mix
3. Topping Mix

Ingredients

SUGAR, FLOUR, STARCH, FAT WITH EMULSIFIERS AND ANTIOXIDANT, BAKING POWDER, FRUIT ACID, PROCESSED SOYA PROTEIN, NATURAL FLAVOURING, STABILISER, COLOUR.

net weight: 8oz 4dr 233g

▲ The EEC is very keen on clear labelling. In addition to the need for information about the ingredients, the consumer also needs to know about food freshness and how clothes should be cleaned. The EEC also wants the unit pricing of goods (how much they cost per kilo) so that customers can see which packet size gives the best value.

▲ This lady has dyed her coat with 'the dye that never runs'. The EEC is soon to pass laws to stop misleading advertising.

► What exactly goes into our food? The EEC is very concerned about food purity and so strictly controls the quality of ingredients, food colourings and insecticides used on food crops.

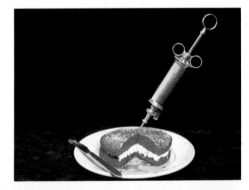

▼ The EEC is very concerned about dangerous toys. The eyes, arms and legs of teddy bears, for instance, are often attached by sharp pins which can injure children if the toy falls apart.

▼ Metal and plastic toys can also be dangerous. Wooden toys are often stronger. Corners can be rounded and there are no sharp edges. The EEC is soon to legislate on toy safety.

The Community and the world

▲ The EEC gives development aid for all sorts of projects in many developing nations. This sign, photographed in the Republic of the Ivory Coast, West Africa, announces that money from the EEC is helping to develop the Republic's palm oil industry.

▼ In 1976, emergency food aid from the EEC to those badly affected by famine, natural disasters or wars involved 50,000 tonnes of cereals, 5,000 tonnes of skimmed milk powder and 3,400 tonnes of butter oil. Emergency aid was given to ten countries. This photograph shows EEC food aid being delivered to people in Ghana.

An interest in world affairs

The foreign policy of the EEC basically has three main aims. First, the desire to improve trading links with other parts of the world; second, the desire to help the developing nations; and lastly, the need to establish better relations with other countries not only in trade but also in other matters. To further these aims, the EEC holds negotiations with different countries out of which come different types of agreement.

Firstly there is an Association Agreement. This was introduced in the Rome Treaty to cater for those countries which were, in 1958, still French, Dutch and Belgian colonies. The idea was that these colonies should benefit from the EEC's internal reductions in customs duties in the hope that this would assist their economic development. When the colonies became independent, the arrangement continued with some changes. New association agreements were signed at Yaoundé in the Cameroons in 1963 and 1969 and then at Lomé in Togo in 1975, though by then other developing nations had also signed the agreements.

The not-so-poor nations and the rich

However, association is not only for the developing nations. It is also open to any state in the world, provided of course that an agreement can be negotiated. The first two countries to take advantage of this were Greece in 1962 and Turkey in 1964. An agreement was worked out between

Greece and the EEC aimed at preparing her for eventual entry into the EEC. This was done in several ways: first, by bringing Greek customs duties slowly into line with those of the EEC; second, by gradually linking Greek and EEC agricultural, trade and economic policies; third, by giving EEC loans to Greek industry.

However, not all countries want formal association agreements. There are also other special agreements. These range from an agreement for commercial and economic cooperation with Canada, to a cooperation agreement with Pakistan, trade agreements with Brazil and the EFTA nations of Europe and an agreement with Romania covering trade in textiles.

The EEC also takes an active part in discussions on all aspects of foreign policy, not just those related to trade. Some features of EEC foreign policy have included support of Britain's policy in Rhodesia, the condemnation of the former regime of the Greek Colonels and an offer of help to China following the earthquake in 1976. A hundred and four nations now have ambassadors accredited to the Community.

Because the EEC has a foreign policy, this does not prevent member states from having their own foreign policies. However, many feel that member states are too independent in this respect and that if all the EEC countries agreed on their foreign policies, they would be more successful in achieving their aims.

▲ Comecon headquarters in Moscow. Comecon — the Council for Mutual Economic Assistance — is Eastern Europe's approximate equivalent of the EEC. It was founded in 1949.

▲ Sir Christopher Soames (in the white shirt), then Vice President of the European Commission, leaving China in May 1975 after trade negotiations with the Chinese.

▼ A meeting of the countries who have signed the Lomé Convention. The Convention, signed in 1975, permits the duty-free entry into the EEC of all industrial and most agricultural products exported by the developing nations who have signed the Convention.

▶ The Soviet Union mistrusts the EEC. It sees the EEC as an attempt to exploit the European worker and create a powerful bloc which can dictate policies to the rest of the world. But Soviet opposition has not prevented communist states from seeking agreements with the EEC. Here, the Romanian Vice President (right) talks with Henri Simonet, President of the Council of Ministers in Brussels in September 1977.

The EEC – yes or no?

The Common Market—good or bad?

It is now over twenty years since the EEC was established yet people are still wondering whether it is a good or a bad thing.

On the good side, supporters of the EEC point out that it has encouraged the peoples of the EEC to work together to solve problems. It has helped them to understand one another's point of view and even sympathize with one another's opinions.

Supporters also claim that the EEC has given the member states a more powerful world voice. However, it has to be admitted that the member states have not taken as much advantage of this united strength as they might. For example, when faced with the Arab oil embargo in the early 1970s, the EEC states, instead of agreeing on a common policy, went their own ways and negotiated individual agreements with the oil-supplying nations.

Prosperity for the people?

On the economic side, there is much disagreement between supporters and opponents of the EEC. Supporters claim that the larger home market has encouraged the growth of industry. As for agriculture, they say that the EEC has helped to make farms more efficient.

People who are against the Common Market complain that it has meant a loss of sovereignty, or political power, for member states. They say that the member states have lost some of the power to control their own affairs because they are now obliged to introduce Community laws, even if they do not like them.

Supporters of the EEC claim that this is nonsense. The member states are all represented on the committees that make the laws. Here they have a right to veto any proposed law which might harm them, and so the loss of political power is quite small.

The rise in food prices

The other main criticism is that the EEC has caused prices to rise, especially in the UK, which has had to scrap its cheap food policy and replace it with an expensive Common Agricultural Policy. But supporters of the EEC claim that more expensive food is a small price to pay for secure supplies and the other advantages which the Market brings.

They also point out that the EEC has not been responsible for all the rises in food prices. Inflation in member states, often caused by wage demands, has been more important, and so too have crop disasters and the weather. Moreover, increases in the world price of foodstuffs, such as coffee, which are not covered by the Common Agricultural Policy, are nothing at all to do with the Common Market.

Deciding on whether the EEC has so far proved good or bad is difficult. People will obviously differ in their views. The best that can probably be said is that the answer lies somewhere between the two extremes.

▲ Yes and no to Europe. The division of opinion at this rally in Trafalgar Square, London, in 1971 is also found in other parts of the EEC. The Danes and the French also have mixed feelings on membership. However, in a referendum on membership in 1975, over 66% of the British people voted to stay in the Market.

▶ Sometimes, member states break the rules of the Common Market and pressure has to be brought upon them to toe the line. Here, Italian wine makers in Rome are protesting against the French government's decision in 1975 to ban the import of Italian wine.

► The May Day parade in Moscow's Red Square. Many people want to see a strong, united Europe as a counterbalance to the world's two superpowers, Russia and the USA. The military threat from the USSR is specially worrying because of the size of its armed forces.

◄ Supporters of the EEC still remember the last war. They remember the suffering caused when the nations of Europe battled with one another. Like Monnet and Schuman and the other founders of the Common Market, they are still anxious that similar wars should never happen again.

► The old aims of the Common Market are still there. The larger home market created by the EEC is supposed to encourage firms to make and sell more goods, so making people richer. This has in fact happened in the six founder member states. Since joining, Britain, Ireland and Denmark have tried to achieve similar rates of economic growth. The world depression of the 1970s has made this difficult.

◄ You cannot please everyone. The EEC has to balance the general interest against the interest of particular groups. Here Dutch dairy farmers protest to a member of the Commission about the low price of milk.

▼ British coastal fishermen protesting against the fishermen of other EEC states being allowed to fish in British waters. The new 200-mile exclusive fishing zone around the Market's shores controls fishing by non-EEC fishermen. But should EEC fishermen be able to go anywhere in the 200-mile zone, or should certain areas be restricted to the fishermen of any one member state? Present EEC rules allow fishermen from other EEC states to within 6 to 12 miles of Britain's shores. If coastal fishing is important to UK fishermen along any particular stretch of coast, then fishermen from other EEC states are only allowed to within 12 miles of that coast.

The future of the EEC

▲ If the member states ever unite into one country, what sort of country will it be? A monarchy, a republic or will it be a federal state like the USA? Who will become Head of State?

▶ In the not too distant future, Spain, Portugal and Greece are expected to join the EEC, increasing its membership from nine nations to twelve.

▼ Belgian Prime Minister Leo Tindemans. In a report published in 1976, he called for greater European unity in the future to strengthen Europe's voice in the world and help solve current economic problems.

Building a new future
Despite the predictions of some people, it seems unlikely that the Common Market will break up. Though the people of the EEC often complain about the Community, it is unlikely that any member state would seriously think of leaving the Market. The evidence is that they still feel that there is much to be gained from unity. Moreover, there is the fear that if any member state withdraws, its authority in world affairs will be reduced. Also, it will face the possibility of still being influenced by the policies of the remaining members, though it will then have less control and influence over them.

New members
In fact, rather than splitting up, the EEC shows signs of growing. In the near future, Greece, Spain and Portugal are likely to join and there are many Norwegians, Swiss and Austrians who would like to see their countries in the Market.

The principle that Greece, Spain and Portugal should join the EEC has been accepted. What remains to be decided is when, and what the terms of entry should be. At present, there are difficulties because the economies of these countries are in many ways backward and rural. They depend very much on the sale of certain crops, such as grapes and olives, which are already abundant in the EEC. Also, industry in the new states will have to be protected for a time from competition from industry in the other member states.

A country called 'Europe'?
We are still a long way from fulfilling the aim of the original supporters of European unity, that there should eventually be a country called 'Europe'. Today, the idea still has its supporters. Some people would like to see member states agreeing in most matters so that all major decisions would be made in Brussels. Others go even further and want to see the EEC become a federal nation like the USA with a strong central government in Brussels and 'state' governments in each of the member countries.

However, other people are appalled at these suggestions. In fact, it would take many years of peaceful cooperation to create such a union.

Even then it is doubtful, because of the strength of nationalist feeling in different parts of the EEC, whether the creation of such a state would be either possible or desirable.

Closer cooperation
What we shall probably see in the future is member states cooperating more and more in all fields, not just in economics. This means therefore that the EEC will become less a purely economic organization. It will become something broader. We shall probably also see an increase in the powers of the EEC. But this will also be accompanied by an increase in the powers of the member state governments where matters relating to their own countries are concerned.

The EEC of the future?

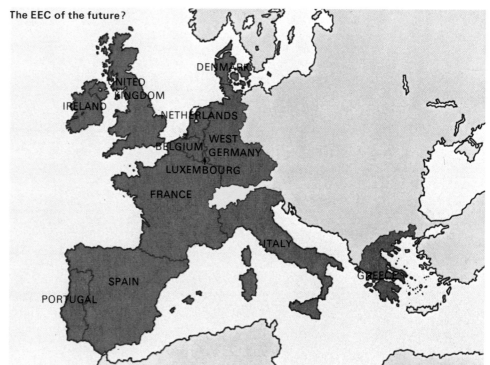

▲ Europe is a long way behind in the space race mainly because of the high cost of space projects. However, cooperation makes expensive projects possible. Ten European nations have so far come together to create the European Space Agency. One of its aims is to put a European 'Spacelab' into orbit by 1980.

► A demonstration by Welsh and Scottish nationalists. The forces of nationalism in Europe are still very strong. The EEC will have to try to reconcile the benefits of unity with the desire of people to govern themselves and to retain their national identity.

UNITED KINGDOM OF
GREAT BRITAIN
AND NORTHERN IRELAND

EUROPEAN COMMUNITY

PASSPORT

◄ The probable design of the British version of the new European Passport bearing the words 'European Community'. The colour also changes from blue to burgundy. As yet, the passport means very little though it could be the first step towards sweeping changes in the nationality laws.

► Rival contender as monarch of Europe? King Juan Carlos seen here with wife of the President of France. He has played a major role in returning Spain to democracy after the death of Franco, so making Spanish entry into the EEC a real possibility.

Reference: *Human and physical geography*

Rainfall

Rainfall
cm	inches
150	60
100	40
75	30
50	20

Temperature

Temperature

°C January Temperature
°C July Temperature

Copenhagen 0°C 17°C
Edinburgh 3°C 14°C
Dublin 5°C 16°C
Amsterdam 2°C 17°C
London 4°C 18°C
Brussels 3°C 18°C
Bonn 2°C 18°C
Luxembourg 3°C 21°C
Paris 3°C 18°C
Rome 8°C 24°C

Climate

On the rainfall map, note in particular the high rainfall in Ireland and in the western parts of the UK and Brittany. Using Dublin as an example, note also the mild winters and cool summers of these parts. Both the high rainfall and moderate temperatures are the result of westerly winds blowing off the Atlantic Ocean. As you move further away from the ocean, so the rainfall decreases, winters become colder and summers hotter.

Rome, in the south, enjoys a Mediterranean climate with mild winters, hot summers and a moderate rainfall which falls mainly during the winter.

Population

The population density map shows how unevenly population is distributed throughout the EEC. Some areas have a lot of people while others have very few. There are many reasons for this. The main reason is that some areas have very little industry and the land is very poor. It is therefore difficult to find a job and so people who live there are forced to move to other areas in search of work. This has important effects on many EEC policies, especially regional policy.

But there are some areas which are still heavily populated despite the fact that it is difficult to find a job. Examples of this are north-eastern England and north-eastern France. This is caused by old industries such as coal, iron and steel, declining, the failure of these regions to attract new industries, and the fact that people cannot or will not move to new areas in search of a job.

▶A map showing where people live in the Common Market. Notice how population is densest in the industrial regions of southern Scotland, northern England, London, South Wales, Paris, Lyon, Milan, Genoa and Florence and the belt of territory extending from Antwerp and Amsterdam in the north, eastwards to the Ruhr and south down to the Rhine Valley. Notice also how the edges of the Common Market are comparatively scarcely populated.

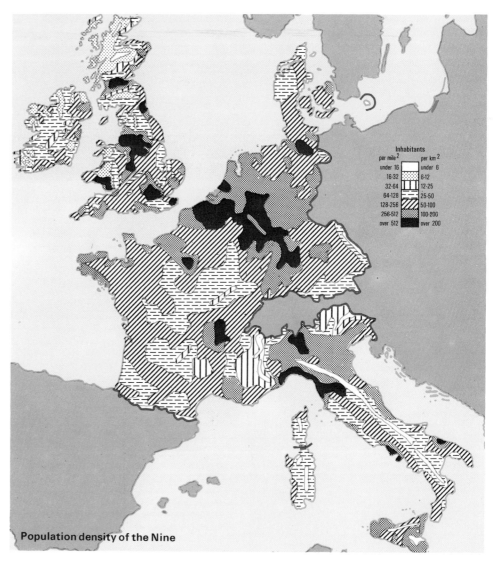

Inhabitants
per mile²	per km²
under 16	under 6
16-32	6-12
32-64	12-25
64-128	25-50
128-256	50-100
256-512	100-200
over 512	over 200

Population density of the Nine

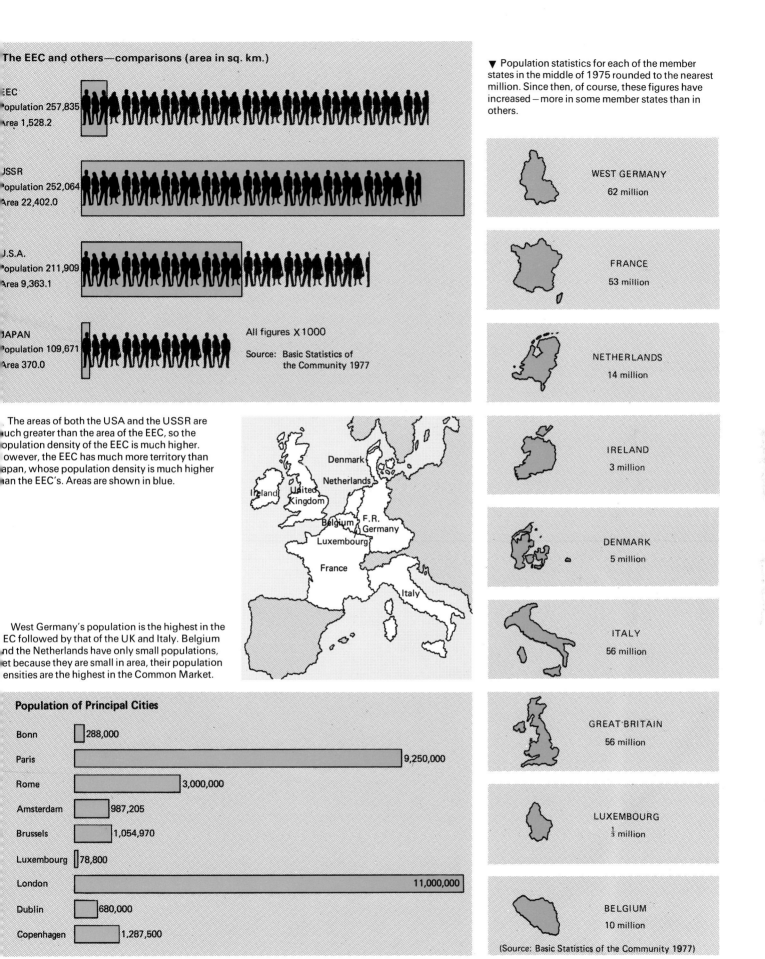

The EEC and others—comparisons (area in sq. km.)

EEC
Population 257,835
Area 1,528.2

USSR
Population 252,064
Area 22,402.0

U.S.A.
Population 211,909
Area 9,363.1

JAPAN
Population 109,671
Area 370.0

All figures X 1000

Source: Basic Statistics of
the Community 1977

The areas of both the USA and the USSR are much greater than the area of the EEC, so the population density of the EEC is much higher. However, the EEC has much more territory than Japan, whose population density is much higher than the EEC's. Areas are shown in blue.

West Germany's population is the highest in the EEC followed by that of the UK and Italy. Belgium and the Netherlands have only small populations, yet because they are small in area, their population densities are the highest in the Common Market.

Denmark
Netherlands
Ireland
United Kingdom
Belgium
F.R. Germany
Luxembourg
France
Italy

Population of Principal Cities

City	Population
Bonn	288,000
Paris	9,250,000
Rome	3,000,000
Amsterdam	987,205
Brussels	1,054,970
Luxembourg	78,800
London	11,000,000
Dublin	680,000
Copenhagen	1,287,500

▼ Population statistics for each of the member states in the middle of 1975 rounded to the nearest million. Since then, of course, these figures have increased — more in some member states than in others.

WEST GERMANY
62 million

FRANCE
53 million

NETHERLANDS
14 million

IRELAND
3 million

DENMARK
5 million

ITALY
56 million

GREAT BRITAIN
56 million

LUXEMBOURG
$\frac{1}{3}$ million

BELGIUM
10 million

(Source: Basic Statistics of the Community 1977)

49

Reference: *Living and working in the EEC*

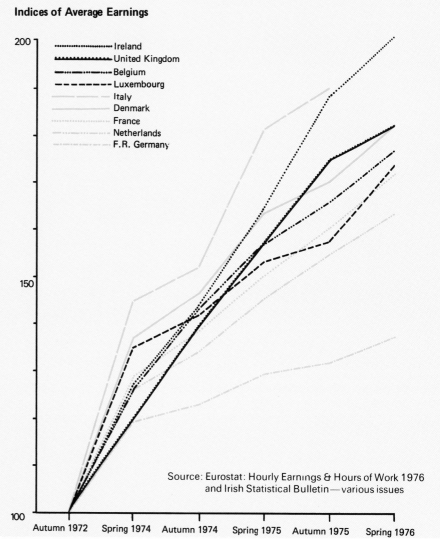

Indices of Average Earnings

- Ireland
- United Kingdom
- Belgium
- Luxembourg
- Italy
- Denmark
- France
- Netherlands
- F.R. Germany

200

150

100

Autumn 1972 Spring 1974 Autumn 1974 Spring 1975 Autumn 1975 Spring 1976

Source: Eurostat: Hourly Earnings & Hours of Work 1976 and Irish Statistical Bulletin—various issues

How wages have kept pace with prices

The graphs show how wages and prices have risen during the period Autumn 1972 to Spring 1976.

On the whole, the graphs suggest that wage increases in the member states have kept up with the rise in prices. Undoubtedly, the trade unions in the Common Market have had much to do with this.

The graphs also suggest that prices are never far behind wage increases.

Since the spring of 1976, however, further information has shown that wages have not kept up with prices. Standards of living have begun to fall as people have found themselves with less money to spend.

The reason for this is not difficult to understand. Since the oil crisis of the early 1970s, the EEC has been plagued by inflation and prices have soared. In an attempt to try and control the inflation, governments have been forced to stop large wage increases which feed the inflation. The result is that prices have gone on rising, but wages have risen more slowly. It is only now that the fruits of this wage control policy are being felt as price increases begin to slow down, bringing price and wage increases more into line.

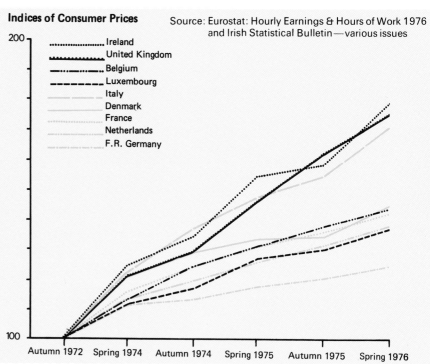

Indices of Consumer Prices

Source: Eurostat: Hourly Earnings & Hours of Work 1976 and Irish Statistical Bulletin—various issues

- Ireland
- United Kingdom
- Belgium
- Luxembourg
- Italy
- Denmark
- France
- Netherlands
- F.R. Germany

200

100

Autumn 1972 Spring 1974 Autumn 1974 Spring 1975 Autumn 1975 Spring 1976

Employment by main sectors.

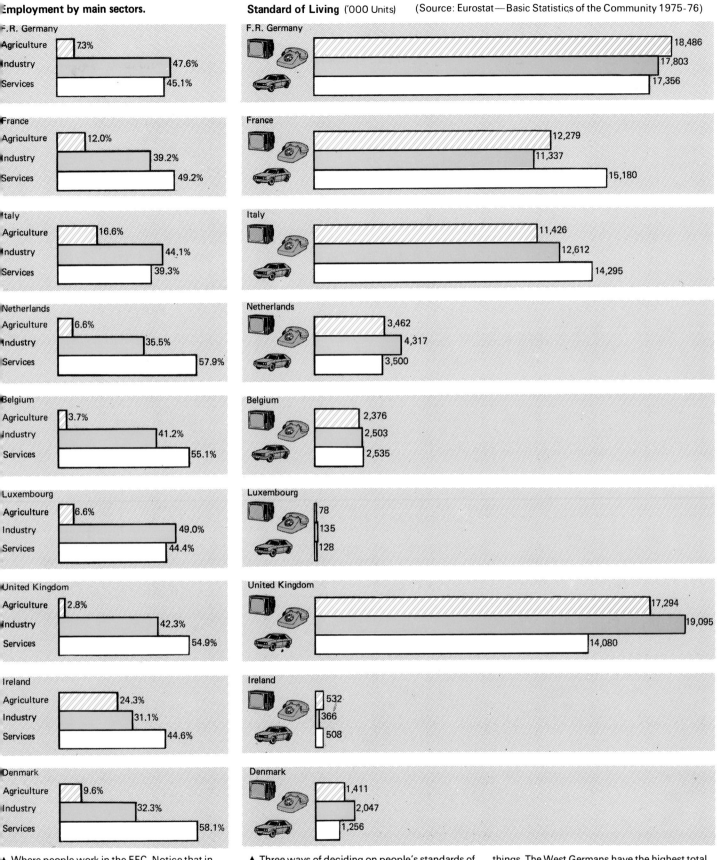

Standard of Living ('000 Units) (Source: Eurostat—Basic Statistics of the Community 1975-76)

F.R. Germany
Agriculture 7.3%
Industry 47.6%
Services 45.1%

18,486
17,803
17,356

France
Agriculture 12.0%
Industry 39.2%
Services 49.2%

12,279
11,337
15,180

Italy
Agriculture 16.6%
Industry 44.1%
Services 39.3%

11,426
12,612
14,295

Netherlands
Agriculture 6.6%
Industry 35.5%
Services 57.9%

3,462
4,317
3,500

Belgium
Agriculture 3.7%
Industry 41.2%
Services 55.1%

2,376
2,503
2,535

Luxembourg
Agriculture 6.6%
Industry 49.0%
Services 44.4%

78
135
128

United Kingdom
Agriculture 2.8%
Industry 42.3%
Services 54.9%

17,294
19,095
14,080

Ireland
Agriculture 24.3%
Industry 31.1%
Services 44.6%

532
366
508

Denmark
Agriculture 9.6%
Industry 32.3%
Services 58.1%

1,411
2,047
1,256

▲ Where people work in the EEC. Notice that in many of the member states, more people work in the service sector, providing services for their fellow citizens, than work in either industry or agriculture. Notice too the importance of agricultural employment in several member states.

▲ Three ways of deciding on people's standards of living. Possession of cars, telephones and television sets usually means that people are fairly wealthy and have money to spend on these comparative luxuries. In the poor countries of the world, such as India, it is still rare for people to have these things. The West Germans have the highest total number of cars, though it is tiny Luxembourg which has the most cars per thousand people.

51

Reference: *Industry*

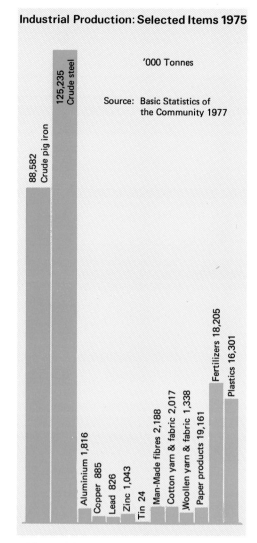

'000 Tonnes

Source: Basic Statistics of the Community 1977

- Crude pig iron 88,582
- Crude steel 125,235
- Aluminium 1,816
- Copper 885
- Lead 826
- Zinc 1,043
- Tin 24
- Man-Made fibres 2,188
- Cotton yarn & fabric 2,017
- Woollen yarn & fabric 1,338
- Paper products 19,161
- Fertilizers 18,205
- Plastics 16,301

Industry in the EEC

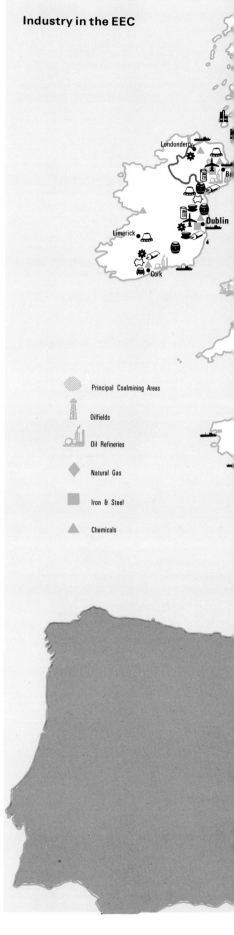

- Principal Coalmining Areas
- Oilfields
- Oil Refineries
- Natural Gas
- Iron & Steel
- Chemicals

▼ The Gross Domestic Product (GDP) of the member states of the EEC compared with those of Japan and the USA. The GDP of a country is the total value of all goods and services produced.

Goods include such things as cars, televisions and building materials. Services include such jobs as postman, teacher, train driver and pop singer. As economies develop, so the GDP increases. But it must be added that rising prices will also cause the figures to increase.

▲ There are three interesting features about the industrial production of the EEC. The first is the wide range of goods produced in the EEC — from very simple to very complex. The second is the rapid growth in industrial output, especially since the establishment of the Common Market. The depression of the mid 1970s has, however, had bad effects, and in 1975 production figures were down on those for both 1973 and 1974. The third is that industry is located in a few specific areas.

Gross Domestic Product: The Nine and Selected countries (European units of Account)

(1 EUA = £0·41)

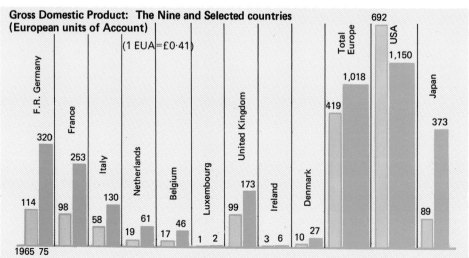

- F.R. Germany: 114 / 320
- France: 98 / 253
- Italy: 58 / 130
- Netherlands: 19 / 61
- Belgium: 17 / 46
- Luxembourg: 1 / 2
- United Kingdom: 99 / 173
- Ireland: 3 / 6
- Denmark: 10 / 27
- Total Europe: 419 / 1,018
- USA: 692 / 1,150
- Japan: 89 / 373

1965 75

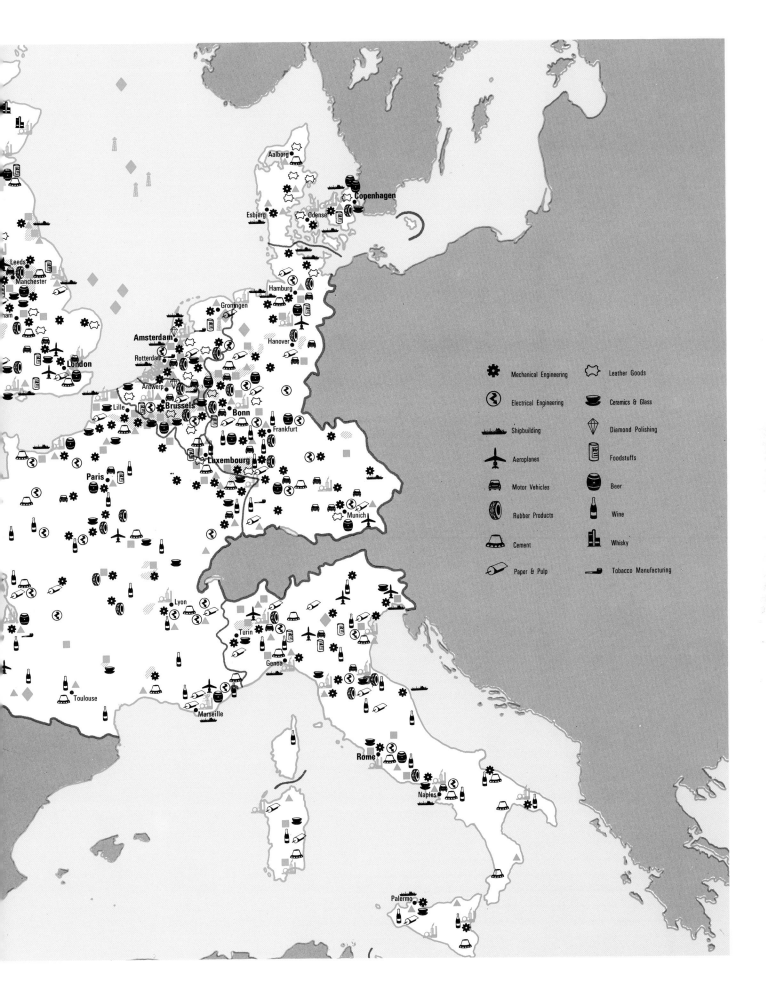

Aalborg

Copenhagen

Esbjerg · Odense

Hamburg

Groningen

Amsterdam
Rotterdam · Hanover

Antwerp
Brussels · Bonn

Lille

Frankfurt

Luxembourg

Paris

Munich

Lyon

Turin

Genoa

Toulouse

Marseille

Rome

Naples

Palermo

Symbol	Industry	Symbol	Industry
Mechanical Engineering		Leather Goods	
Electrical Engineering		Ceramics & Glass	
Shipbuilding		Diamond Polishing	
Aeroplanes		Foodstuffs	
Motor Vehicles		Beer	
Rubber Products		Wine	
Cement		Whisky	
Paper & Pulp		Tobacco Manufacturing	

Leeds
Manchester

am

London

53

Reference: *Agriculture*

Agricultural production in the Nine
('000 Tonnes)

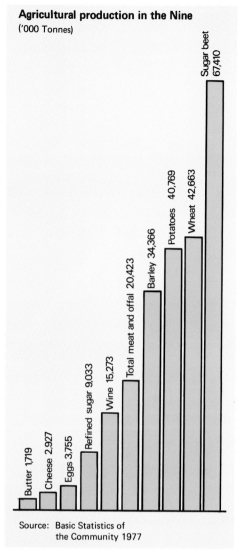

Butter 1,719
Cheese 2,927
Eggs 3,755
Refined sugar 9,033
Wine 15,273
Total meat and offal 20,423
Barley 34,366
Potatoes 40,769
Wheat 42,663
Sugar beet 67,410

Source: Basic Statistics of the Community 1977

Londonderry
Belfast
Dublin
Limerick
Cork

Cattle

Pigs

Sheep

Principal Fishing Ports

▲ Common Market agriculture produces a wide variety of produce. Hardy cereals such as oats thrive in the harsh climate of the north of Scotland, while fine dairy produce comes from the lush pasture land of the Netherlands and Denmark. Delicate grapes are a feature of many different parts of the Continent, and the British are even starting to grow them.

The Common Agricultural Policy covers most of the produce from the Common Market's farms. It covers grains, rice, fruit, vegetables, plants, flowers, flax, hemp, hops, tobacco, wine, beef and veal, pigmeat, poultry, fish, eggs, milk products, oils and fats. The main exceptions are mutton, lamb and potatoes. Also, imported agricultural produce such as tea and coffee is not covered.

▼ The Common Market is gradually producing more food as production methods improve. Improving the efficiency of agriculture is a slow process. In many parts of the Community it involves asking farming communities to change habits and methods which they have used for generations. In some cases, however, it involves encouraging people to leave the land, land which their families may have farmed for many centuries.

If agricultural policy is to be humane and take the needs of the people into account, it will take many years to bring about changes such as these.

Agricultural output of the EEC (Indices of agricultural output. Average 1961-'65 = 100)

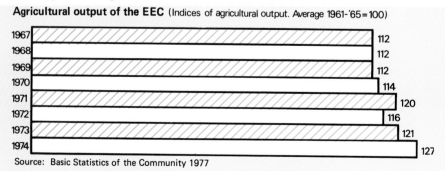

1967 — 112
1968 — 112
1969 — 112
1970 — 114
1971 — 120
1972 — 116
1973 — 121
1974 — 127

Source: Basic Statistics of the Community 1977

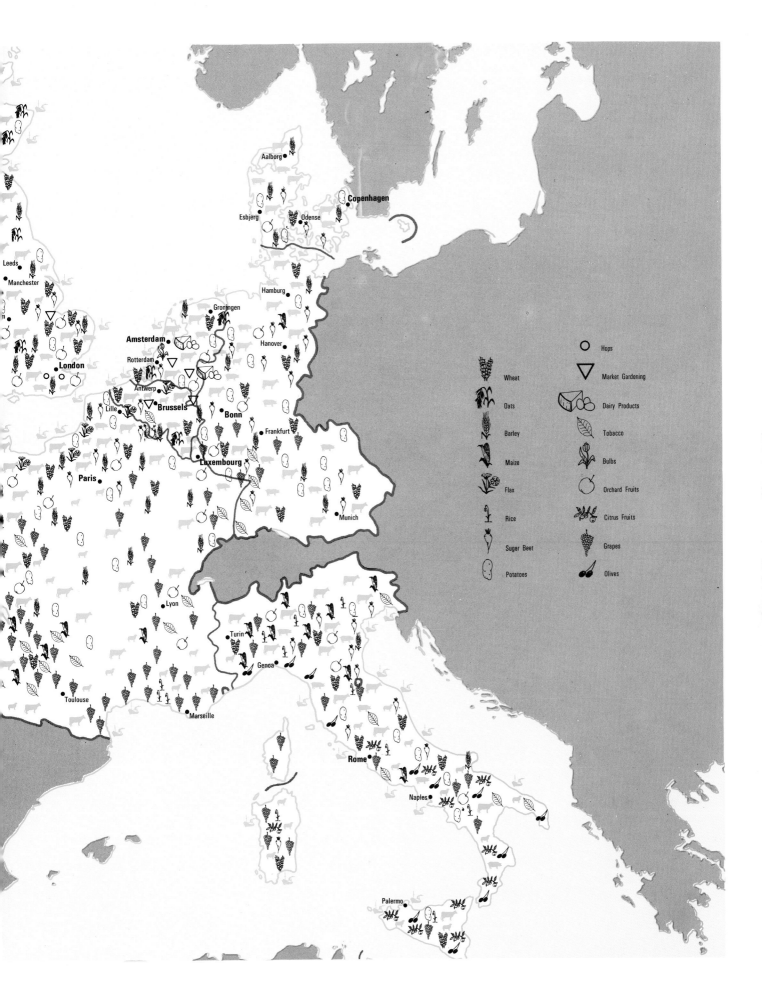

Leeds
Manchester

Aalborg

Copenhagen

Esbjerg   Odense

Hamburg

Groningen

Amsterdam

Hanover

Rotterdam

London

Antwerp

Brussels

Lille

Bonn

Frankfurt

Luxembourg

Paris

Munich

Lyon

Turin

Genoa

Toulouse

Marseille

Rome

Naples

Palermo

	Hops
Wheat	Market Gardening
Oats	Dairy Products
Barley	Tobacco
Maize	Bulbs
Flax	Orchard Fruits
Rice	Citrus Fruits
Sugar Beet	Grapes
Potatoes	Olives

Reference:
The Community and trade

▼ Since the barriers to trade within the Community were removed, trade between the member states of the EEC has increased. From 1958 to 1972, the six original members of the Community increased their trade with each other by 724% — from £3,536 million to £29,120 million. In 1958, 27% of their trade was with each other, while in 1972 it was 52%.

Critics of the EEC argue that trade between the member states of the EEC would have increased anyway, and that the establishment of the Common Market therefore had little effect.

However, various studies tend to disprove this. One such study, that of Williamson and Bottrill in 1971, showed that by 1969, trade in manufactures between member states was over 50% higher than it would have been if the EEC had not been formed.

Since joining, the United Kingdom's trade with the other Community countries has increased, and at a rate faster than the increase in her trade with the other countries of the world. Overall, the United Kingdom imports more from the other EEC countries than she sells to them. But the latest figures show that the gap between imports and exports is closing as British firms begin to take advantage of the opportunities that the EEC offers.

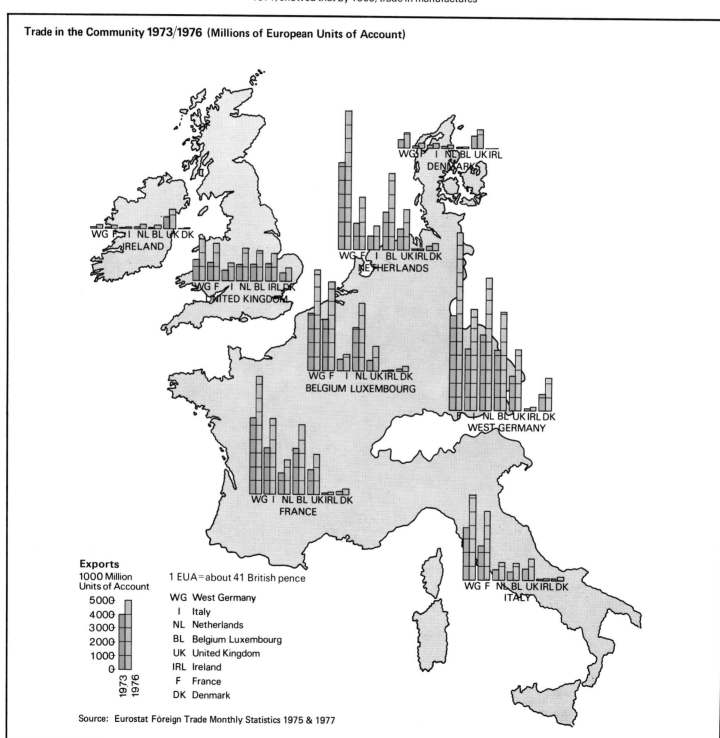

Trade in the Community 1973/1976 (Millions of European Units of Account)

Exports
1000 Million Units of Account

5000
4000
3000
2000
1000
0

1973
1976

1 EUA = about 41 British pence

WG West Germany
I Italy
NL Netherlands
BL Belgium Luxembourg
UK United Kingdom
IRL Ireland
F France
DK Denmark

Source: Eurostat Foreign Trade Monthly Statistics 1975 & 1977

The EEC and world trade

The EEC is the world's largest trader. It is the USA's single largest trading partner and the world's major importer of goods from developing countries. It has important trade relationships with the oil producing states of the Middle East and important commercial ties with the developed economies of Australasia, Canada, Japan and South America. Commercial links with China and the Communist countries of Europe are small but growing.

Encouraging world trade

The Treaty of Rome pledged the EEC to encourage world trade by gradually abolishing all restrictions on international trade – in particular by the lowering and removal of customs duties. The EEC has fulfilled this pledge in various international negotiations that have taken place. By the end of 1974, EEC customs duties were on average 1.1% below those of the USA and Japan. A long list of goods can now be imported duty free into the EEC by all nations. The overall effect has been to make it easier for countries to export goods to the EEC with the result that the total volume of world trade has increased.

Special agreements

Special association and trading agreements between the EEC and other nations have also encouraged trade. For instance, agreements signed in 1974 with the members of the European Free Trade Association (EFTA) have meant that by 1977, about 300 million people in western Europe were benefiting from free trade in industrial products.

Similarly, the Lomé Convention, signed in February 1975, allows the 46 developing nations who signed the Convention to export duty free to the EEC most of their agricultural and industrial produce. This not only encourages growth in world trade, it also contributes to the economic development of the nations involved.

However, critics may argue that the Common Market, along with other developed nations in the world, is still not doing enough to help both the trade and the economic development of the Third World.

▶ How the trade of the EEC developed during the period 1967-1975. Notice the steady increase in both imports and exports. Notice also the fall in imports and the very small increase in exports in 1975 caused by the start of the world economic depression.

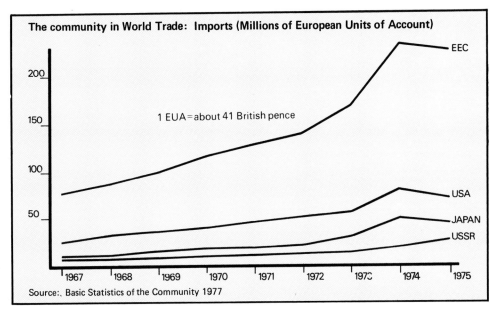

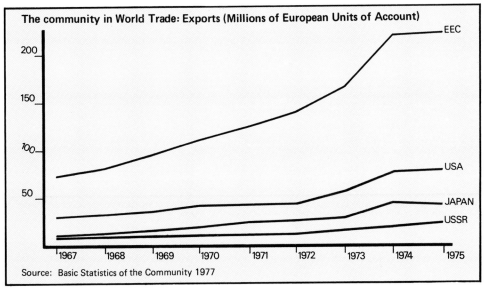

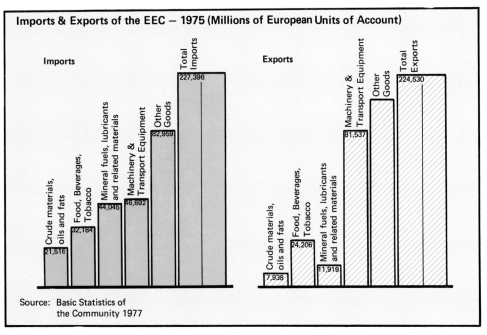

A brief history of the EEC

MAIN EVENTS IN THE HISTORY OF THE COMMON MARKET

1946 September. Winston Churchill, speaking in Switzerland, suggests the idea of 'a kind of United States of Europe'.

1947 June. American Secretary of State, George Marshall, proposes that US aid should be given to Europe to help recovery. The Americans ask Europeans to cooperate to decide how the aid can best be used.
October. Belgium, the Netherlands and Luxembourg join together in an economic union known as Benelux.

1948 March. The Brussels Treaty is signed by Benelux, France and the UK. The countries agree to help one another in the event of attack.
April. 16 European nations set up the Organization for European Economic Cooperation (OEEC). This encourages cooperation between members in economic matters, especially in the distribution of American aid.

1949 April. 10 West European nations, together with the USA and Canada, establish the North Atlantic Treaty Organization (NATO). Member states agree to come to one another's aid in the event of an attack.
May. The Council of Europe is established by 10 West European states to promote the discussion of all matters of common concern except national defence.

1950 May. The French Foreign Minister, Robert Schuman, proposes the setting up of the European Coal and Steel Community (ECSC). This will place Europe's coal and steel under a common authority.

1951 April. The Treaty of Paris establishing the ECSC is signed by France, West Germany, Italy and the Benelux countries.

1952 May. The same six countries sign a treaty establishing a European Defence Community. This means a common army for the Six. The Treaty does not come into force because the French Parliament does not agree with it.

1955 June. The Messina Conference of the Foreign Ministers of the ECSC countries. This sets up a committee under Paul-Henri Spaak to study ways of achieving greater unity in Europe.

The Six

1957 March. The work of the Spaak Committee results in the signing of the Treaty of Rome, establishing the EEC. A second treaty, signed at the same time, establishes the European Atomic Energy Community (Euratom).

1958 January. The Rome Treaties come into force. Walter Hallstein becomes the first President of the Commission.

1959 November. Britain and six other non-EEC members establish the European Free Trade Association (EFTA).

1961 August. Britain, Ireland and Denmark make their first application for membership.

1962 April. Norway makes its first application for membership.

1963 January. Negotiations to enlarge the Community are stopped after de Gaulle vetoes British entry.

1967 May. Britain, Ireland and Denmark re-apply for membership.
July. Norway re-applies.
November. De Gaulle again objects to British membership.

1968 July. The customs union is completed, 18 months ahead of schedule. Tariffs on trade between member states are now completely abolished and the Common External Tariff is enforced. The last remaining restrictions on the free movement of workers are also abolished.

1969 July. Georges Pompidou becomes President of France.
December. The Heads of State of the EEC member countries agree to complete, enlarge and strengthen the Community.

1970 June. Negotiations on British, Irish, Danish and Norwegian entry begin in Luxembourg.

1971 June. Negotiations between the EEC and the applicant states are successfully concluded.
October. The British House of Commons accepts British entry into the EEC by 356 votes to 244.

The Nine

1972 January. The Accession Treaty (Treaty of Brussels) is signed by the UK, Denmark, Norway and Ireland.
April. The French people vote in a referendum to allow other countries to join the EEC.
May. In a referendum, the Irish vote by a large majority to join the EEC.
July. The Norwegian people vote not to join the Common Market. Norway withdraws.
October. The Danish people approve Danish entry in a referendum.

1973 January. The Treaty of Brussels comes into force. François Xavier-Ortoli becomes President of the Commission.

1974 February. British general election. Labour wins and promises to re-negotiate the terms of UK entry into the EEC. Labour promises to put the results of the renegotiations to the British people in either an election or a referendum.
April. British Foreign Secretary James Callaghan begins the re-negotiations in Luxembourg.

1975 June. A referendum is held in the UK to decide whether Britain should remain in the EEC. The people vote by a two-to-one majority to stay in the EEC.

1976 January. Publication of the Tindemans Report. This calls for greater European unity.
February. The Council of Ministers declares that it is in favour of Greece joining the EEC. It suggests that talks with Greece should begin.
September. The Council of Ministers agrees that direct elections to the European Parliament should be held everywhere in the EEC on the same day in May or June 1978.

1977 January. A new Commission, headed by Roy Jenkins, takes over.
March. Portugal officially applies to join the EEC.
July. The last remaining customs duties between the original six members and the three newer members are repealed. This completes the establishment of a customs union between all nine members.
July. Spain formally applies to join the EEC.

Glossary of terms

Council of Europe This was established in May 1949 by ten West European states though others have since joined. Its headquarters are in Strasbourg, France, where its fine, new building is also used by the European Parliament. The aim of the Council is to encourage European cooperation and understanding, in particular by regular meetings of representatives of the member states. On the whole however, it is just a glorified 'talking shop' and has no real power or influence.

Council for Mutual Economic Assistance (Comecon) Eastern Europe's roughly equal to the EEC. It was set up in 1949 by seven East European states including the USSR plus Outer Mongolia to link their economies so that they would become self-sufficient. It was suggested for instance that Romania should specialize in agriculture. The Council also encourages cooperation in scientific research and technology.

Council of Ministers This is composed of nine ministers, one from each of the member states of the EEC. Member states take it in turn to hold the Presidency of the Council for six months. It is the Council which has the final say on whether or not a proposal should become law. Although in theory decisions are by majority vote, in practice all ministers and therefore all member states have to agree before a proposal becomes law.

Court of Justice This is composed of nine judges, one from each member state, all appointed for six year renewable terms. Decisions of the judges are by simple majority. The Court may stop EEC law being broken and punish offenders. It may be asked to interpret EEC law and it may act as an appeal court.

Customs union or common market A customs union is established when countries decide to remove all barriers to trade between them such as customs duties. At the same time, they establish around themselves a common customs duty which they apply to all goods entering the union from non-member countries. The EEC is a customs union or common market.

Economic and Social Committee A 144-member body representing employers' organizations, trades unions and other interests including consumers in the EEC. Its job is to advise on proposed Community laws.

European Atomic Energy Community (Euratom) The Treaty establishing this was in fact signed at the same time as the Treaty establishing the EEC. There are therefore two Rome Treaties. It was set up by the member states of the EEC to encourage cooperation in the development and peaceful use of nuclear energy. On their entry to the EEC, the United Kingdom, Ireland and Denmark also joined Euratom. Its governing bodies are the same as those for the EEC and the ECSC.

European Coal and Steel Community (ECSC) This was established in 1951 by the Treaty of Paris. Belgium, France, Italy, Luxembourg, the Netherlands and West Germany decided to create a common market in coal, steel and iron. These products could be traded anywhere in the market and they would not be subject to customs duty. There was to be a 'high authority' or central government to govern the coal, steel and iron industries of the member states as one industry. The ECSC had a separate Commission, Parliament and Court of Justice though these were merged in 1967 with those of the EEC and Euratom.

European Commission The term can be used in two ways. First it can be applied to the 13 Commissioners who are the senior 'civil servants' of the EEC. They are responsible for suggesting legislation and then once it becomes law, for seeing that it is enforced. Commissioners are appointed by member states. The larger states appoint two Commissioners each and the smaller states each appoint one. Once appointed, Commissioners do not serve national interests but the Community interest as a whole. The Commission has a President, at present Roy Jenkins. There are also five Vice-Presidents. Ordinary Commissioners serve four-year renewable terms while the President and Vice-Presidents serve two-year renewable terms. The term is also applied to all the staff employed in the Berlaymont building and elsewhere who work directly for the Community.

European Communities This is the term used to describe the three European organizations, the EEC, the ECSC and Euratom which are governed by the same European Commission in Brussels. In practice, it is difficult to distinguish when it is the EEC, ECSC or Euratom that is conducting a policy. They used once to have separate Commissions, Parliaments and Courts of Justice but these were merged in July 1967.

European Economic Community (EEC) or **Common Market** as it is popularly called. This was set up by the Treaty of Rome signed on March 25 1957. The Treaty came into force on January 1 1958. The original members, known as the 'Six', were Belgium, France, Italy, Luxembourg, the Netherlands and West Germany. In 1972, by signing the Treaty of Accession in Brussels, Britain, Ireland and Denmark also joined.

European Free Trade Association (EFTA) This was established by the Stockholm Agreement of 1959 as an alternative to the EEC. Seven European nations, the United Kingdom, Austria, Denmark, Norway, Portugal, Sweden and Switzerland agreed that manufactured goods could be traded duty free between them.

European Parliament At present, it is composed of 198 members appointed by the national parliaments of the member states. It meets in either Luxembourg or Strasbourg for one week every month to discuss the business of the EEC. Basically, its only job is to consider all proposed EEC laws and to deliver opinions about them. It therefore has only limited powers. It can however dismiss the Commission and now has the final say on the Budget. Its powers though are likely to increase when its membership increases to 410 and when it is directly elected by the people of the EEC.

European Unit of Account (EUA) Nine different currencies are in use in the nine member states of the EEC. It makes life very difficult if every time a sum of money is mentioned in an EEC document, this sum has to be given in nine different currencies. So the EEC has invented the Unit of Account and all sums of money are expressed in it. In June 1977, 1 EUA = about 41 British pence.

Further reading and information

The European Parliament
The London office of the Parliament is housed in the same building as the Commission, but the telephone number is different (01-229 9366). It will help with pamphlets and other information on the workings and activities of the Parliament. It is of course possible to visit the Parliament in session in either Luxembourg or Strasbourg. There are visitors' galleries and debates can be listened to by using simultaneous translation. The London office can supply details.

The Council of Europe
This will provide teachers with free copies of all its publications on topics of European (not just EEC) interest. Full details may be obtained from the Division for General and Technical Education, the Council of Europe, 67006 Strasbourg, Cedex, France (61.49.61.).

Special help for teachers
The Schools' Information Unit of the Centre for Contemporary European Studies at the University of Sussex, Brighton BN1 9RF (0273-66755) offers help to teachers dealing with Europe. It will provide advice on the curriculum, teaching methods and resources. It produces many useful publications, including the periodicals *Teaching About Europe* and *Exploring Europe*.

In addition to the Sussex unit, certain other establishments also offer help for teachers. These include Bulmershe College of Higher Education, Reading, Avery Hill College, London and St Martin's College, Lancaster.

Teachers should also be aware of the activities organized by the European Association of Teachers with 30,000 members throughout Europe. The UK headquarters are at 20 Brookfield, Highgate West Hill, London N6 6AS (01-340 9136). Teachers can join the association for a modest fee. It organizes conferences and provides various services for members. The publications of the UK section include the journal *The European Teacher*.

Other sources of help
There are 37 European Documentation Centres throughout the United Kingdom which house all EEC publications including the Official Journal. The problem is that neither the material in them nor their organization make them suitable for children. Details of the nearest EDC may be obtained from the Commission.

There are also a few local information centres in various places dealing with the EEC. These are run either by volunteers or by the local council. Details may be obtained from the European Movement.

Finally there are the embassies of the member states. Many of them will provide free information sheets and speakers to talk to children and adults.

Books and other materials
Books for children on the EEC are regularly reviewed in *Teaching About Europe*. Readers should however note three books – E. Barker *The Common Market* (Wayland 1976), B. P. Price *The New Europe* (Macdonald Educational 1977) and G. Dinkele *Our Common Market Neighbours* (Longmans 1975). The latter can be used in conjunction with this book because it develops in greater detail many of the issues introduced by our text.

Adults wishing to further their own knowledge of the EEC may start by looking at D. Swann *The Economics of the Common Market* (Penguin, 1975). For help with the economic and political jargon surrounding the Market adults can consult the *Penguin Dictionaries of Economics and Politics*. Teachers wishing to teach about the EEC can get help in course design from M. Williams *Teaching European Studies* (Heinemann Educational 1977) and further bibliographical data can be obtained from P. Freeman and H. Nicholas *European Studies Handbook* (Longmans 1977).

The European Commission
You can write, telephone or visit the information offices of the European Commission. The main office is at 200, rue de la Loi, 1049 Brussels, Belgium. In the United Kingdom, there are offices at 20, Kensington Palace Gardens, London W8 4QQ (01-727 8090); at 7, Alva Street, Edinburgh EH2 4PH (031-225-2058) and at 4, Cathedral Road, Cardiff CF1 9SG (0222-371631). In Ireland, there is an office at 29, Merrion Square, Dublin 2.

These offices will supply free leaflets on the Community. Though most of these are intended mainly for adults, many can be used by children and young people, especially if an adult is on hand to explain them. You can also ask to be put on the mailing list to receive a regular newsletter called *European Community* and press releases and background notes. These keep up to date with events in the EEC. Schools and similar institutions can also obtain free slide sets and hire, free of charge, 16 mm films dealing with the Community.

The Anti-Marketeers
A number of anti-Market organizations have come together to form the National Council of Anti-Common Market Organizations. Along with member organizations, the National Council publishes a variety of brochures and handouts including its own magazine *Secession – the British Journal of Anti-Common Market Operations*. Full information can be obtained from the Council's address at Hayes, Kilmersdon, Bath (07613 2207).

▲ The London Office of the European Commission at 20, Kensington Palace Gardens, London, W8 4QQ.

The European Movement
This is the main pro-EEC pressure group in the United Kingdom. You can join the movement for a small fee. It has local branches in many parts of the country which organize regular meetings. The Movement puts out various publications, again mainly for adults, including a regular news sheet called *Facts*. The Movement will arrange for speakers to come and address groups of any age on different European topics. The address is Europe House, 1A, Whitehall Place, London SW1A 2HA (01-839 6622).

Index

THE COMMON MARKET (E.E.C.)

Member countries of the Common Market are shown in dark colours

	International Boundaries
■ ◉ ◎ ○	Cities and Towns
	Railways
	Main Roads
✈	Airports

Scale 1:12,000,000

200 miles

200 kilometres

100

100

0

0

0

100

Projection: Miller Oblated Stereographic

ARCTIC   OCEAN

Barents   Sea

White Sea

Murmansk

Arkhangelsk

Volga

U. S. S. R.

Vitebsk

Smolensk

Leningrad

Pskov

Minsk

FINLAND

HELSINKI

G. of Finland

Riga

Vilnius

Kaunas

Tampere

Kaliningrad

Luleä

Gulf   of   Bothnia

BALTIC   SEA

Narvik

STOCKHOLM

Tromsø

SWEDEN

NORWEGIAN   SEA

Göteborg

Malmö

Trondheim

Kattegat

Aarhus

COPENHAGEN

NORWAY

OSLO

Skagerrak

DENMARK

Flensburg

Kiel

Bergen

Stavanger

NORTH   SEA

ARCTIC   OCEAN

Denmark   Strait

Arctic Circle

GREENLAND
(Denmark)

Faroe Is.
(Denmark)

Shetland
Is.

Aberdeen

Dundee

Edinburgh

Newcastle

Leeds

Hull

ATLANTIC

Glasgow

UNITED

Belfast

Liverpool

KINGDOM

OCEAN

DUBLIN

IRE

ICELAND

REYKJAVIK

Arctic Circle

4 5 6 7 8 9 10 - IL - 88 87 86 85